How To Change Your Mindset and Rewire Your Brain

Christopher Rothchester

Table of Contents

Introduction

Have you ever wanted to change who you are, like a moth to a butterfly? Well, that starts by rewriting your mind through methodical steps. The million-dollar word to consider is: Neuroplasticity. What that big college exam word means, is the ability of your brain to re-energize synaptic connections through learning. The root word, Neuro, is derived from the words 'Nervous System.' Plasticity comes from 'plastos', a Greek word for moldable. Hence, the nervous system has a moldable brain and Neuroplasticity. It's to create connections and pathways between neurons. This highfalutin term was introduced by Polish neuroscientist Jerzy Konorski not long before the Titanic sank in 1906. As a writer who has experienced symptoms of anxiety overthinking and was once tested to have ADHD, these are some awesome tips and tricks to help remedy some of those situations.

First, let's learn a bit about the brain. Within the brain are 100 billion neurons. It's only in the last 10 years did medical scientists learn that the brain grows well into the adult years. So the question is, how can you grow your brain through neuroplasticity? It all starts with the hippocampus, the memory cortex part of the brain. Twenty years ago, there was evidence that listening to Mozart's Sonata can increase one's IQ. So in the state of Georgia, everybody born was given a Mozart album to listen to in Georgia. The result: no change in IQ. What that is called, according to neuroscientist Richard Haier, is the schmozart effect. Meaning: it has been thoroughly debunked as quackery. What you can do, is the little thing in this book to develop your brain. The question is, can an old dog be taught new tricks? Short answer: Yes.

In the 1890s psychologist, William James theorized that the brain is not changing into adulthood. It's fixed. He wrote that organic matter has a tough degree of plasticity which means, he thought, one can't change much once they reach adulthood. Just like the above Mozart album, that trend was debunked in modern times. Decades later, in the 1920s Karl Lashley, a researcher found that neural pathways within Rhesus Monkeys—a break thought was formed in science in the understanding of the changes in the brain and Neuroplasticity. Then in 1960, a team of researchers studied people who had strokes and then were able to regain the usage of a limb again like magic. Which revealed a new fact: the brain grows and is malleable into adulthood and can rewire itself to learn.

There is a lot of medical and scientific information here, and chances are—well—you're not a doctor. But in layman's terms, it is documented that most neurodegenerative diseases harken from degenerative loss of neuroplasticity. Some of the usual suspects with mental illness are tied to that tweaking, such as Alzheimer's disease, Parkinson's disease, and Huntington's disease. This guide will give a step-by-step approach to how you can improve your brain through a series of techniques. From learning about turning a negative into a positive to a little thing called emotional intelligence. So let's begin our adventure into consciousness growth or mindset shift.

Or… maybe helps you get a bit better at Wordle.

Chapter 1: Using Neuroplasticity to Success

First things first, neuroplasticity is the strengthening of neuronal pathways in your brain. This book will avoid using platitudes and attempt to get into the nitty-gritty of how to improve your brain. Let's start at the beginning. At birth, a baby has 2,500 synapses, but by age three, there are 15,000. These tiny things in the brain are tiny gaps in between neurons where the nerve impulses system communicates. By using various techniques, it improves your mind's malleability so you can retain more info and be more efficient at doing it. This is called synaptic plasticity. This is the ability of your networks in your brain to reorganize through new information and rewire differently than it was before, so you are more adaptable to doing it.

Example: You never studied the topic of the ancient Rome colosseum, and then you gotta do a book report on it, and then talk about it fluently? Then will help one expand the plastic in their brain. Doing Out Of Comfort Zone things, again and again can improve cognitive functions and improve your ability to learn and even get better at your day job. One wants a malleability brain that can adapt to new things on the fly and not be settled by the same repetitive behavior.

The conscious and subconscious work hand and hand, according to Sigmund Freud. According to recent research, 'rewriting' your brain can have huge changes in your life and can spearhead improvement. So what does that word mean exactly? Well, it's using science to my shrewd and repetitive new patterns to create positive results. Thanks to the understanding of science and Brain chemistry, when you were once 'set in your ways,' you can become anew. Gradually, though embedding that pattern into your subconscious, it becomes second nature. According to

Michael Merzenich, who is a renowned neuroscientist at the University of California, your mind likes to filter what it can remember and then ignore stuff it doesn't want to remember, and one should refocus attention on their goals.

One does not need to do aggressive mental gymnastics like astrophysics or trigonometry to grow their brain. Just thought-provoking repetition in a positive manner. A person's unconscious also develops neurons by doing tasks to stimulate the mind. Day by day, if you continue to work at something and strive to be better at it, it will one day slowly change your life like a metamorphosis to a butterfly. The two main definitions of neuroplasticity:

1.1 Functional Plasticity

This first one isn't related to just 'getting smarter' but is more actually related to damage. When a brain is damaged, maybe by accident, and can rewire that part of the brain to a new one. When you once couldn't move your right hand due to a terrible collision through therapy, perhaps you'll be able to move that hand again.

Structural plasticity This is when the brain can change its structure through malleability by simply learning. When your brain is dominant in one area, through repetition and hard work, your brain structure can change through hard work. Couldn't play the violin? Maybe, a few months from now, you can go through that little thing called Structural Plasticity.

Some of the things that can happen when you are knowable with Neuroplasticity:

- Learn new things and retain that information

- Become even better as current skills by enhancing cognitive skills
- If having a stroke or traumatic brain energy, one can recover quicker
- Improves areas in the brain that are slowing down through the passage of time and/or fight against developing Alzheimer's
- Using Improvements that can boost your mental agility and brain fitness

With the more complex terminology out of the way, let's get more to common tongue nonmedical language.

First, let's learn a bit about the different types of neuroplasticity so you can, well, get smarter and grow your brain even more. The first is functional plasticity, the mind's ability to move if there is a damaged area in the brain or other areas that aren't hurt. On the other hand, structural plasticity is the brain's structure and acute changes from the ability to learn. The most important part of this book is the ability to learn. What that does is improves your Brain-Derived Neurotrophic Factor. A child's brain develops neurons at an astonishing rate up until three; learning about it can help develop your mind for the betterment of yourself. Using this technique will help you overcome or (being honest) lessen the symptoms of panic, anxiety, depression, overthinking, and ADHD. Within some of the following tips, you learn how to rewire your brain to just retain more information and be more apt to get out of your comfort zone and... live a little more boldly by using the little thing called Neuroplasticity.

There are many things one can do to improve your neuroplasticity, but here are seven of them. For example, you, in theory, can be a total introvert and then be an extrovert by simple brain plasticity enhancements. Diametrically the opposite, From one extreme to the other. A real-life example of that would be tongue-wagging free-throw dunking former NBA Superstar Michael Jordan. Who, while playing basketball in North Carolina, had an Achilles Heel, the main weakness in his game. That was: he couldn't dribble well, according to Teammate Kenny "The Jet" Smith would then say was dribbling. Well, the next time he saw him, he became a vastly better ball handler where that weakness in his game could not be exploited. "The only guy whose weaknesses became his strengths." That is a prime example of physically getting better at something, dribbing, but the same rules apply to mentally getting better too.

Without further ado, here are some tips to light millions of pathways up in your brain.

1.2 Steps How To Improve Neuroplasticity

1. Mental Gymnastics - Challenge yourself. Whatever you want to do in life, maybe it is being an astrophysicist, learning to be a gardener, doing something that challenges you, and working at it and thinking about it—often. It doesn't have to be anything big or daring, but something out of your comfort zone. Depending on your age, maybe start doing things accessible and easy and work your way up. But do something that is thought-provoking. Crossword puzzles change to, but so does complex writing on things like neuroplasticity, for instance. What you want to do and look at your Achilles' heel or your general weakness, use grit and determination to strive to be better at that. There are studies that highly successful people put forth 15 to 30 minutes a day to just--think and assess new information that they got. What that little bit of time does is helps you plot your next move like a game of

chess. But some of the time, there are more scientifically proven things to improve your brain.

2. Running

According to the Epidemiological evidence from the National Library of Medicine, exercise improves Neuroplasticity and helps ward off Alzheimer's Disease.

Whenever your blood is pumping in aerobic activities, you can increase the Neuroplasticity in your brain. What this does is it will improve your cognitive and motor function in your brain so you can expand your horizons and get that much better at things. This is also said to help best, hippocampus for memory and learning. The other silver lining of this: you could help ward off dementia. Simply sprinting can boost your Brain-derived neurotrophic factor, AKA BDNF, which is a key molecule in the plastic altercations in the brain. Things like memory and learning are tied to this. Some good exercises are running but also weight lifting, aggressive sports, and dancing, but the more physical heart-pumping exhausting, the better... like sprinting. Other things exercise does for cardiovascular health is, Lower blood pressure, Help regulate blood sugar, Reduce asthma symptoms, Reduce chronic pain, Aids sleep, Regulates weight, Strengthen the immune system, boost mode, reduces risks of falls, and last but not least Improve brain power for Neuroplasticity.

3. Make Art

From research in 2015, it was found whenever you do art; there is a positive behavior change in the brain. Frontal white matter is reorganized whenever you do something artistic. You don't have to be Michelangelo's creating the Sistine Chapel to consider yourself an artist. Start doing basic things, basic noodles, writing projects, or paintings and you can both improve your outlook on life but also help neuroplasticity in your brain. Painting, for instance, improves Cortical and cerebellar activity whenever you get better at drawing. Doing art doesn't just improve your brain; it helps you self problems, reduces depression, and helps with relaxation. You are just limited to visual art, creating music also has been proven to promote neuroplasticity. According to research, it improves memory, prevention, and motor skills and causes the age-related decline of the brain. In the day and age of the internet, there are tons of ways to learn how to compose music, paint, and draw. The first destination for people on a budget and limited time: Youtube. Another idea: apps. For learning to play guitar, the gold standard app is Yousician.

4. Learn a Second Language

According to the National Library of Medicine study, learning a second language can have positive changes in White-Matter Connectivity. It brings greater strength to the brain's connectivity between regions in the brain. You can learn a new language at any age to help improve your mental acuity, vocabulary, ability to multi-task, and creativity skills. Many apps can make learning a new language, well, not exactly easy, but the easiest it's ever been. Duolingo is an app from all stores that makes learning Spanish with childlike simplicity and colorful graphics. But it's about being persistent and determined to retain the info and keep at it, it is what will make you truly get positive Morphological brain changes.

5. Read and Learn Everyday

The United States is ranked 125th on the global literacy ranking. There are many states where the budget is distractedly different for adult education to get people to learn. In this competitive world, reading, and reading every day on your passion topic can be a deciding factor in your growth. Not only reading but make a calculate an effort to learn every day and open-minded to things that you may not initially be excited by but through an open mind, this becomes more interesting to you. Many of the chapters give information on how to retain new info, sleeping, exercise, the eating right, but one has to have an unbridled passion for learning every day. One has to be in a frame of mind of continuous learning. Also, not just in familiar topics, too. If your weakness is not knowing ___ then study up on ___ until you are adept.

6. Sleep

This is consistent with one-third of a person's life and is critical to brain plasticity—-among other things. As everybody with half a brain knows, a healthy amount of z's is essential for energy restoration and also your immune system. If you want to learn how to play the violin, instead of putting in long hours and cutting your sleep back, make sure you get your proper 7-9 hours of sleep. Things to watch for: make sure you get the proper REM sleep, and this can roughly be tabulated by Smart Watch. Various studies prove just how vital sleep is to not your brain but also your entire body. TED conference on Youtube with a professor of neuroscience/psychology Matt Walker. During it, he gives hard truths about how critical sleep is. Including health, retaining info & creativity.

7. Meditation

 Magnetoencephalography Studies that there is a correlation between meditation and neural plasticity. Another thing that can be done is using simple Vipassanā, the Indian word for 'insight,' using meditation. There are many types of meditation, and they consist of mindfulness meditation, from spiritual meditation to focused meditation movement. Both the easiest ones for starter meditators would be mindful meditation and spiritual meditation (prayer). For the former, one just has to close their eyes, remain still, and have pleasant and empty thoughts go into your head. Stuff like focusing on the quietness of there or your own heartbeat. That drowns out energy-draining, overzealous thoughts and helps both reduce anxiety and help ward off Alzheimer's and depression, but at the same token, breath boosts your brain's ability to learn. The first thing to learn with meditation is simple breathing exercises like Diaphragmatic breathing. The first: is the 4-7-8 breathing technique.

8. Ketosis (Fat), DHA (Found In Fish Oils)

This is a high-fat diet contestant with low carbs. It's used to control epilepsy in children, but more than that. Typically, the brain uses glucose from carbohydrates for energy in the body. But when you avoid eating those foods and start fasting, the body enters into the fat and is broken down into what is called ketosis. The body starts using fatty acids from a molecule named Beta-Hydroxybutyrate. What this does is improves Long-Term Potentiation (meaning, increase the strength of nerve impulses along pathways). Essentially, subscribing to the Mediterranean diet and basically eating healthier, and getting more omega-3 found in fish royal into your system, can help you learn. Studies say that Omega-3, a fatty acid found in fish, can improve neurogenesis. Eating a good amount of this can help your brain development and muscle activity and also cell growth. According to the National Library of Medicine, it helps develop synaptic plasticity in the brain. There are other benefits of heating seafood: it prevents cell death from antiapoptotic effects and the imbalance of free radicals and antioxidants within one's system, called anti-oxidative stress, and helps reduce inflammation. In Layman's terms: it does a lot for the mind and the body.

9. Magnesium

As noted, instead of your key ingredients to help your brain from some scratchy wonder pill from Dr. Oz, get it from eating leafy foods. Studies say that a healthy amount of maximum improves the visual cortex in mice. It is also tied to hundreds of biochemical reactions in your body, like anti-inflammatory benefits and cognitive function. This is part of a critical physiological role in the development of the brain. Again, it is best to eat food like vegetables, dark green in color, grains, milk, and yogurt instead of popping a wonder pill.

10. Reduce Stress

Neurogenesis has found some startling facts: Chronic stress can hinder the neuronal adoption needed to improve your brain. This form of stress causes neurons in the brain to change, either shrink or grow. It reduces the hippocampus and prefrontal cortex's ability to have positive neuroplasticity. Furthermore, chronic stress can alter spine destiny and dendritic length, and this branches into the prefrontal cortex. So if you are a person that gets proper sleep, with no substance abuse problems, exercises, and still has a hard time remembering... it might be because your brain is in a fight or flight response from stress. So if you have a high-stress job, which many people do, meditation or a midday jog to help reduce the stress and improve the circuitry of the brain.

11. Fast

Intermittent fasting is documented to improve brain cognitive performance, according to the National Library of Medicine. What it does is it helps increase the Brain-derived neurotrophic factor (BDNF) and, from some estimates online, by 50% to 400%. According to Mark Mattson at the National Institute on Aging, it can delay Parkinson's and Alzheimer's. However, starving yourself for long periods has the opposite effect. The key words are intermittent fasting. Mattson argues that our genes are from our ancestors who did have 3 square meals a day plus a nice snack. Rather, our bodies were built to go into occasional fasting mode, and our brain reacts accordingly.

12. Travel

One doesn't need to go to Bangladesh to consider that traveling either. It is all about going out of your comfort zone. Consider venturing on a troll to a nice safe area you never walk to, going shopping somewhere else, or simply going on a hike. Studies say that traveling can boost your BDNF levels and your cognitive flexibility. The reason: you are out of your element, and your brain is forced to create new synapses faster. There also is what is called Virtual Travel, where you can see different places on YouTube if you are really walking there. Essentially, to improve your brain, you should avoid following the beaten path every day that does not develop your brain and broaden your way of thinking.

13. Eating Right/Turmeric Curcumin

According to the National Library of Medicine, this orange-in-color spice can to wonders for your Hippocampal Circuits and Attenuates. This Ayurvedic medicine has been used for centuries in Middle Eastern and Asian countries. A study was conducted on rats with depression, and this powder helped reduce symptoms of it. Also, Curcumin Alters Neural Plasticity for the improvement of the brain. During clinical trials testing people with MDD, Major Depressive Disorder/ Curcumin can help reduce it. But it certainly wouldn't hurt to try to improve our brain using these. However, if you really want to improve your brain, you have to do a variety of things and not just put spice in your food. The other more simple thing to do is just eat better sustenance. Best example: is the Mediterranean diet. Filled with fish, nuts, bread, fruits, vegetables, and little red meats or artery-clogging gut-busting processed food.

1.2 Summary

This is a variety of medically proven ways to improve the plasticity of your brain. To help slow down cognitive decline, the sooner you practice better brain health, the more likely you will have a fresher brain as you get older. According to the Alzheimer's Association, Age, family history, genetics, and other factors like an injury to the head or healthy aging. But formulating a strategy to now just improve your brain for job performance but to avoid certain degenerate diseases is vital to your health.

Chapter 2: A Winner's Belief System

Tom Brady is widely considered the greatest football player of all time. He has a whopping seven Super Bowl rings and is still playing as a starting QB into his 40s. Even if you negate the seven Super Bowls, that is still quite the accomplishment to still be playing. He had trust in the system with Bill Belichick and, afterward, Bruce Arians. What he has is a quintessential winner's belief system. A mindset to overcome adversity and become the best at his profession. If you are looking to pattern yourself off of a winner's mentality—-it starts with good building blocks and a positive attitude. Have a powerful belief system within yourself, unshakable, unbreakable, and incorruptible, and you will be on a pathway to significant self-improvement. There are ways that if you visualize an ideal version of yourself, maybe years from now, and then start to just walk, talk and act like that person... you will eventually become that person. A winner's mindset like Tom Brady's stems from an innermost belief in one's self, the system he worked in, and steady improvement and listening to constructive feedback. The reason is what you think dictates our behavior. Here are some points of self-improve that could fundamentally change who you are for your own welfare. But the best thing that could help: check your ego at the door.

2.1 Steps How To Develop a Winner's Belief System

Growth Mindset - Having the mental state that your brain is a sapling looking to grow as tall as a 250-foot ancient tree that is a couple of thousand years old tree called General Sherman. Meaning there is a ton of growing one can do even when reaching adulthood. Your mind needs to grow, and if you already think you are great and something, chances are that you will have a harder time getting even better. Writers, in particular, at a young age want to think they are the next Stephen King, and they push away all negative feedback because they have made up their minds. What they have done has put them in a fixed mindset that hinders their growth potential. Always stay in a young sapling frame of mind.

2. Get Out Of Your Comfort Zone

Following the same repetitious path is not going to develop you develop your skills. Learn to get out of your usual parameters. Just like with weight lifting, where if you do the same workout, the muscle memory learns, and then it's harder to make gains. If you start doing other workouts to work for different muscle groups, just like the mind, you can grow again. Tackle Fear and uncertainty of newness as a way to live life. Go into uncharted waters (not dangerous ones, of course. No rock climbing without a harness, for instance). Think of new adventures as a way to live life and not fear. The aforementioned Tom Brady did the exact same thing when he went from New England to Tampa Bay. In the wise words of Morgan Freeman in The Shawshank Redemption, "Get busy living or get busy dying."

3. Formulate a Winning Strategy

Simply mapping out in your mind, or maybe in a journal, a way to achieve your goal to be an astronaut, or whatever, is your first step to actually being one. Formulate something through preparation and mental fortitude. Whatever your dreams may be, having a strategy for the way to get them is the pathway. Research the winning strategies in your field. Perhaps, duplicate the same methodology of someone else. Improvise. Or, if you're using anything involving technology, embrace the latest forms of technology and the Internet. Also, sometimes (usually) some things may take longer than expected. If one has a winning strategy, it may take time, but perseverance is your greatest ally. Be your own Bill Belichick.

4. Have a Contingency Plan

On the flip side of the strategy, the more pessimistic side, make sure and have at least some form of contingency plan in case things do not go exactly according to plan. Sometimes plan B can open the doors to plan A. This next part does contradict the idea of having a positive outlook, but it's still good to be prepared in case something does happen . There is this thing called Murphy's Law. The first rule is, Anything that can go wrong will go wrong. The second rule: Nothing is as easy as it looks (also pessimist). Finally, the third rule is: Everything takes longer than you think it will. Though all of these are pessimistic attitudes, it's always good to have at least some type of backup plan in case the worst does happen.

5. Seek to Be an Expert

One has to be realistic, but one can be an expert in many fields when one puts forth maximum effort and grit. It is nature versus nurture. The age-old question... or both? For some professionals, there is a ton of nature, meaning you're born with many skills or physical attributes that help you do this job better. But on the other side of the coin, there is a nurturer where if you do enough of a certain professional in the off hours and put forth perhaps thousands of hours into it, get a degree; you may become an expert. The major * on this segment: artistic endeavors and sports careers are extraordinarily difficult to become an expert at. Those two professions are a healthy dose of born with it nature versus standard nurture professionals like becoming a volleyball coach. Whatever your dreams may be, go for it.

6. Focus, Focus, Focus, Focus

In the day and age of TikTok, crying kids, apocalyptic politics, and tons of streaming content, there are innumerable ways to be distracted from your endeavors. But the difference between someone who can achieve their goals and not: is a razor-sharp focus. Eliminate distractions and have a 'me time' where you can focus on your lofty ambitions each and every day... preferably at the same time every day, creating a habit. For instance, most writers, in particular, create an iron-clad routine where they write every day at the same time. Stephen King, for instance, writes the same 2000 words every day, 7 days a week. I'm not saying you have to have a Herculean work ethic, but if you just have to focus on that bull's eye every day, step a little closer each day... you got a leg up on your competition.

7. Embrace Change

Bob Dylan has a song The Times Are A-Changin'. Truth be told, time is always in flux, so one has to learn to adapt to change. Another quote, "The One Most Adaptable to Change is the One that Survives." By Charles Darwin. Embrace change and handle it in stride. Not only that, realize without a little change from the beaten path, things can be a little dull. As noted in the neuroplasticity chapter above, embracing change isn't just a winning mindset; it's a way to prove your mental acuity. So instead of being habitual with a thing like you are under mental enslavement, realize you have free thought to do whatever you like (legally) in order to grow your mind and, in a competitive spirit, be a winner.

8. Don't Be a Sore Loser

If you've heard the expression before, to know how to win, one must know how to lose... and sometimes many times. If you lose too graciously, and not just in sports, but have setbacks in life, do not lose motivation. The Iconic politician Winston Churchill had a quote on this, "Success consists of going from failure to failure without loss of enthusiasm." Elon Musk's SpaceX had 3 rockets that failed before its fourth one launched and was the first privately-developed rocket in orbit. If first, you don't succeed, try, try, again through practice and determination. One of the positive things about losing is giving you a second chance at it using all the knowledge you acquired to try it again and again. If one keeps proper tenacity even when they get a bad deck of cards, they may be able to win the race through sheer willpower. So when you redouble your effort, renew your strategy, and spearhead forth with confidence and might, you might see just the W the next time.

9. Be Flexible and Calm to Change Strategy on the Fly

This is a microcosm of what you can do on the fly with your chips down. Michael Jordan was losing with seconds to go in the 1998 NBA finals he kept his composure. The score was 85-86, Jazz with the lead with 37.1 seconds left. The crowd in Salt Lake City was on their feet, cheering and on pins and needles of suspense. What Jordan did, as John Stocking passed the ball to Karl Malone Jordan recognized they were running the same play in the paint in the lost post. So Jordan remembered that, with catlike agility, he came to Malone's blindside and stole the ball from him like a bandit and dibbled out the court with calm. With seconds to spare, Bulls coach Phil Jackson did not do a time so the Jazz could not set up the defense. His Airness the ball and slowly dribbled up the court to each up the most time on the clock. With the clock ticking down, Michael did a cross-over on Bryan Russell and the topic of the free-throw line and shot the ball. Swish. Only 5.2 seconds remained and used his mental fortitude and made the game-winning shot. The most famous shot in NBA history was made. All of this is a strategy for how you can completely change your strategy to win as long as you keep your composure and mind open for the winning game plan.

10 . Competition Is a Good Thing

Speaking about competition, if you have somebody who can inspire you in some fourth of competition, be it a writing partner, fellow salesman, or maybe a salon owner, you can use competitors to reach an even higher echelon. Competition is a good thing. If you are a person who wants to be a master in some type of field—-or maybe even competent, have somebody who can play off to maximize your performance. A good example would be Bulls player Scottie Pippen got to play with Michael Jordan. They practiced together. And went against one another in scrimmages. Though MJ is generally considered the GOAT, the greatest player of all time, he also helped Scottie Pippen reach the zenith of his potential by working with MJ and seeing the dedication, work ethic, and, most of all competitive spirit he brought forth in every game So if you are a rookie in your field, or an intermediate, look to that top dog in the field to inspire you to use as a competitor motivator. It may not happen overnight, or maybe never, but the competition will make you better at your craft than if you were left in solitude. Anybody you can feed off of can help you strive for your best.

11. Find a Winning Team

"Great teamwork is the only way we create the breakthroughs that define our careers." - Pat Riley. If you don't have a team, or at least some type of person, that can coalesce around, it is going to be challenging to reach your pinnacle. Depending on your career, writing, for instance, which is a job of solitude (usually), you still do indeed need some time of 'team' to reach the furthest potential (an editor, publisher). If you indeed rise up to the ranks in your very lone wolf professional—-at the end of the day, you will be in a team. Because even a lone-wolf job or personality needs constructive feedback from a team to reach that apex. Francis Ford Coppola wrote the screenplay for The Godfather, but he also collaborated with Mario Puzo. Then he worked within a team to find the best people and hired Al Pacino and Marlon Brando. WW2 mathematician Alan Turing worked with a team to break the Nazis' U-Boat Enigma. All jobs, solo jobs, and team jobs, eventually lead to teamwork and interpersonal skills. So whatever professional there is you yearn for, learning to work within a team is crucial to the macrocosm of things.

12. Research the Best

The Baddest Man on the Plant, Mike Tyson, was idolized by Muhammad Ali. Oprah Winfrey said her inspiration was Maya Angelou. Steve Jobs saw Polaroid entrepreneur Edwin Land as his hero. Whatever your modus operandi is with your career and your life, find a beacon of light to strive for. Because chances are, there is somebody out there who did the same profession first at the high caliber you could pattern your game plan after. One could research not just their career, but their (usually) humble beginnings to draw inspiration from. For many iconic people, there are innumerable books about learning from their success. For entrepreneurs, it might be advised to read "Steve Jobs" by Walter Isaacson. Or for painters, another one by the same author Leonardo da Vinci. Everyone has a calculating strategy to become better at their job than anybody, even if not in a profession where one can find untapped inspiration from. Every iconic person had to start at some time at the bottom to reach the uppermost ranks of their career. The first stepping stone would be to go to your bookseller, focus and read about them. They formulate a game plan using many of their techniques. Simple? No. Possible. Yes. If you wanna be a winner, study them.

13. Everyday Goal Oriented

Being a person with strong decision-making skills for 'the bigger picture is one step to changing your mind. By meticulous planning and organization, having self-awareness, keen time management, and detailed research and analysis of your objective, you are on a path to self-improvement. Whatever your life, astronaut, teacher, whatever, if one plans ahead and bit by bit heads towards that goal, you will be that much closer to achieving your goal. Moving closer to your lofty finish line takes using many methods but one of the keys is the aforementioned. Have a goal ahead of yourself, and in the same token of breathing, keep an optimistic mind frame. It's less about having some overnight success like winning the Powerball Jackpot; that is a Pipe-dream. It's more about heading straight and narrow towards a goal day by day. When it comes to the ups and downs of goals and how hard it is to achieve, Jerry Seinfeld said it best, "Keep your head up in failure and your head down in success."

14. Love/Be Passionate About Your Job

Finding something that that you actually enjoy helps lubricate the ball bearing to achieve your dreams. Everybody has had jobs they dislike, and those jobs are harder to find meaningful growth at. What that thesaurus type word to describe this is: passionate. It is to have a strong passion or belief for something that is the momentum for you to tackle your goals. If you're a person that dislikes writing, for instance, you can use some positive thinking and learn to enjoy sometimes Herculean endeavors of writing. Find a professional that you are passionate about, and that will be the great stepping stone to going places.

15. Being Thankful

Be thankful for what you have and take heed of what others may not. Having a sense of graciousness and a respectful person just helps cut down on some unforeseen variables: hostility. Which in effect, may give you stress and then in a chain reaction, distract you from your ultimate objectives in life. Being a Negative Nancy or a Negative Ned (or whatever they'd call the male version) of what you have and the people around you will have the opposite effect on your aching goals. Simply being thankful for what you have, and having a benign attitude to the people around you, can help build relationships and can both make you happier and also help you spearhead your goals.

16. Toughness

Achieving goals is a long row to hoe. What that takes is vigilance and determination working hand and hand. Whenever there is something that throws you a loop, I have a contingency plan that even if things go haywire, you have a way to continue to press forward to your goals. There are many hurdles one will have before one ultimately achieves, but it is a matter if you have the courage and conviction to continuously jump those hurdles, no matter how many, which is what distinguishes the winners from the losers. Bite your lower lip, and tough it out, soldiers.

17. Find a Guiding Light

Everybody has some hero. Be it Pablo Picasso, Martin Luther King, or Oprah Winfrey. The more humble the beginning of the hero is mixed with great achievements and a remarkable source of inspiration. If you have the desire to become the next great songwriter, then it's probably advised to study up on the true greats like Bob Dylan and Stevie Wonder. Or your inspiration in life can be somebody you personally know like a life coach or a parent. It is crucial to achieving goals by not just working at them, fighting throw ups and downs and zigs and zags, but also having a meaningful source of inspiration to use as a guiding light in the darkness.

18. Stay Fit, Stay Healthy

Your physical prowess correlates directly with your mental acuity. Stay in great physical condition—or at least the best you can in your situation; eating right and excessing can have direct cause and effect on your ability to grow and get that much closer to surmounting that mountain. If your body is not exactly firing on all cylinders, you are kind of in a defensive survivalist mindset, and it's harder for the main person to retain new information— much less have the motivation to head into murky waters and to learn new things. Attempt to take good care of your body, and what you put into your body, be it harmful substances, processed foods, or too much red meat, and you can have a leg up and help your mind. On a final note: the Mediterranean diet in addition to exercise, is a good one to punch to improve health.

19. Read Books

In a 2021 Pew Research survey, they found that 38% percent of Hispanic adults, 25% of Black adults, and 20% percent of white adults haven't read a book in any form in the last year. Those figures are almost triple from 1978. So if you are looking to get a leg up on your competition in the workforce, and naturally improve your mind and critical thinking skills, read books. Not just helpful guide books about neuroplasticity and brain development, but all kinds. From reading about the Ukraine War or Stephen King's book or Tony Robin's book—-all of this ties into developing your mind like a maestro conducts in the orchestra. From the MRI scan from the National Library of Medicine, that brain reading ability Brain maturation, and the circuitry become stronger and obviously more sophisticated. On the other side of the coin, people that didn't read were revealed to have less gray mattering in their brains. Various studies found a relation between the literary level and the gray and white matter in the brain. The moral of all this medical data and percentages is if you're looking to truly develop yourself, follow all of the aforementioned things but read, read, read.

20. Reduce/Eliminate Alcohol

According to the national institute of alcohol abuse and alcoholism, there are damaging effects on the brain and the more widely known cirrhosis of the liver. Drinking too much alcohol can hinder your memory after only a few drinks. Drinking too much over a long period from alcoholism can have lingering effects on the brain. It is reported that 80% of alcoholics delve into what is called Wernicke where they have a deficiency of thiamine, aka vitamin B. What this does is cause confusion and paralysis of the nerves. Over 80 or 90% of alcoholics develop Korsakoff Syndrome which is coordination, walking, and lastly, memory issues. Through brain–imaging techniques research has shown that alcoholics also hinder the growth of new brain cells. The positive twist on all of this doom and gloom: according to them, one year of abstinence shows some improvement from these lingering effects of alcoholism. Of course, there are other substances, marijuana, and all hard drugs. But research shows that all of these are doing something to the brain that will hinder your ability to grow your mind.

2.2 Summary

If you want to be the next Serena Williams, Tom Brady, or LeBron James, put in the blood, sweat, and tears and believe that you have the ability to be great. There are a lot of references to sports athletes in this chapter, and there is a reason why for them to win, they have to overcome the adversity of the swings and momentum of the game. In every single competition, game one has to have confidence, and the ability to overcome potentially losing, or coming from behind to win. And to seal the victory, you have to have a razor-like focus and ability to press on even if it looks like a losing game. If one thinks of a game a lot like a game, and sometimes you win, sometimes you lose, you keep pressing forward through positive thinking... you formulated a winners mentality.

Chapter 3: Turn a Negative Into a Positive

Neuroscientist Rick Hanson wrote in his book Buddha Brain, has a great analogy for this strange quality of the mind. "Your brain is like Velcro for negative experiences and Teflon for positive ones. Simply changing your mind from a negative frame to a positive feed can be a real difference between nailing a big job interview or just being too jittery and not confident to get one. One of the life lessons one could learn from that statement is that all phases of life turn negativity into positive energy and reign in negative thought patterns. There are many techniques that could help control the whirlwind of negative chronic worry of dark thoughts in the head. Having dark thoughts dominate your thinking will prevent you from growing to reach your maximum potential. According to psychologist Scott Bea, PsyD, there is a correlation between negative thought patterns and such mental issues as obsessive-compulsive disorder, anxiety, depression, and chronic worry. Teenagers, in particular, are stricken by habitual negative thinking. So if one is taught how to turn that ship around by reaching out about it or telling a son or daughter about it sooner, it could give them a happier youth which could blossom into a better adult. The moral of the factoid: unchained negative thoughts can make you bonkers.

The other big elephant in the room: is the little thing called negativity bias. One hundred twenty thousand years ago, this was a good thing to have when men hunted with spears were famished for food, or were chased by a rhinoceros. Negativity in the modern world, where you have the necessities at your disposal, chances are if you purchase this book, it means that a lot of negativity is not necessary for your survival. Do you want a little more motivation to squish those Negative Nancy thoughts? How about this. From the year 2004 to 2012, there was a study of seventy thousand women. John Hopkins and published in the American Journal of Epidemiology found that if you have a chipper attitude, more optimistic you have a significantly lesser risk of dying of major causes of early demise. Things such as:

- Heart disease
- Stroke
- Cancer (including ovarian, lung, breast and colorectal cancers)
- Infection
- Respiratory diseases

Some other benefits of just turning that smile upside down, and having a more positive frame form mine are also:

- better quality of life
- higher energy levels
- better psychological and physical health
- faster recovery from injury or illness
- fewer colds
- lower rates of depression
- better stress management and coping skills
- longer life span

Which transitions to the game plan to fix this dilemma of being plagued with doom and gloom thoughts. Having a simply more sunny side outlook on things will make your brain learn better but also adapt to new information better and, most obviously, make one more happy. See, in your amygdala and limbic system in the brain, we are hardwired to notice threats. In these prehistoric times of early man, our brains worked hard to have the maximum focus to not get speared by a wild bull. But in the centuries that have passed, the dangers to use are more trivial.

Losing a job. The girlfriend is angry. Maybe the Chicago Bulls lost multiple games. You can't find your phone or more serious things like a health scare. But generally speaking, the stuff they worry about makes no difference if one is stressed about it or not. Proof? According to research at Cornell University, 85% of Worries Never Happen. Of the 15% of worries that were reality, 79% of the time, people handled those situations. This translates to this hard-hitting number: 97% of our worries are pointless. In a day and age, we have 50,000 thoughts and images each day. So what can one do to help shepherd the dark ones so one can change their mind? Through measured progress, and noticing when you are ruminating in a morose web of thoughts, you can improve your psyche. These are some crucial tips to help commandeer that worst-case scenario type of thinking or in medical terms Cognitive Distortions.

3.1 Steps How Ways to Turn a Negative Into a Positive

1. Positive Mindset - There is this quote by Greek philosopher Heraclitus, "Day by day, what you choose, what you think, and what you do is who you become." Thus, Your thoughts control destiny. If you build yourself up with a positive framework. and tackle negativity with a positive psyche, you can overcome obstacles faster and slowly turn yourself into a more idealized version of yourself. It doesn't just begin with doing a lot of physical work or hours at the office or in a gym, it stems from a mindset of positive thinking. Remove negative self-talk. One of the things this also does is help reduce stress. There is a litany of things that come from just being the good sport of this thing called life. According to the Mayo Clinic, it improves a range of things in your life. First, a positive mindset increases life span and decreases depression/distress/pain. Your body's natural killer cells

have put forth a greater toughness to diseases. The no-brainer part, you will have a superior psychological and also physical body and superior cardiovascular health from disease and stroke. Lastly, reduced the risk of death from cancer, respiratory conditions, and infections. There probably is a saying you've heard dozens of times, but there is a deeper truth to it if you think about the psychological ramifications of it in the long term. So instead of thinking of that glass as half empty, think of it as half full.

2. Keep Positive People Around You - If you have people around you that are dragging you down, be it just not having a goal, substance abuse problems, or just plain 'ol Mean Girls, then you gotta find another crew. If you cocoon yourself around people that can pull you up, put their egos and insecurity aside, and they can help you become a happier person and maybe help you fulfill your goals. Avoid hanging around narrow-minded people, and find people that are open-minded. There is a saying that goes, "You are who you hang around with." That saying rings true. Here is a quote from motivational speaker Tony Robbins, "If we surround ourselves with people who are successful, who are forward-moving, who are positive, who are focused on producing results, who support us, it will challenge us to be more and do more and share more. If you can surround yourself with people who will never let you settle for less than you can be, you have the greatest gift that anyone can hope for." – Tony Robbins

3. Being Mindful of a Cauldron of Negative Thoughts - Emily K Lindsay, is a PhD researcher from the University of Pittsburgh, and John David Creswell from Carnegie Mellon University is another researcher studying mindfulness attention. The two

of them created a MAT, Monitoring and Acceptance Model. Which is to be more turned into one's thoughts and where they are leading one. Though according to their research, you are not going to actually stop negative thoughts. What it does is it helps you through meditation and remedy the situation to normalcy quicker. So when you are in a jam mentally, study up on good meditation techniques or breathing exercises to help lessen those symptoms. The first thing to learn: Mindfulness-based stress reduction.

4. Write a Journal - What this does is instead of being plagued with negative thoughts of whatnot, you have your own writing in your own words of positive things going on in your life. You can have a positive journal of things to be grateful for. But the other thing is what Abraham Lincoln called hot letters. Where he would write an angry letter cooking with a cauldron of emotions, but... not send it. What that does is release the pinup negative thoughts and forms release. So one has two options they can do. But in terms of positive thinking, the first start might be the gratitude journal.

5. Not Everything Negative Is Your Fault - This is basically when within pitch-black catacombs-like situations in life, you blame yourself. But not everything is within your control, and it's best not to jump to a Summary. Just having a positive framework of thoughts and being taught to put the blame on yourself, you will have a better collection of positive thoughts. Self-Blame during such things as a traumatic event is another thing to avoid and will only exacerbate your negative thoughts and personal development.

6. No More Catastrophizing - This is when you go on a plane west, and you think the plane will lose both engines and crash

into the Grand Canyon. It's predicting the worst-case scenario when pushed out of their cozy little comfort zone. What this does is it gives your mind and body undue stress for most likely random ho-hum activities, but it just hinders the way you can grow (or the distance you can travel). Put a lasso on those terrible thoughts, stop suffering, and put forth a positive framework that the worst possible thing that could happen is highly unlikely to happen.

7. Believe in a Positive Scenario - If you are shooting a free throw in basketball, and you already think it is not going in before you shoot... it probably is not going in. But if you, before you even shoot, tell yourself this is saying this is going in... the basketball is more likely to go in. It's because positive thinking lubricates positive outcomes. You learn to trust yourself. So if you go on a big date, and you think positively, and keep your charm, perhaps that date will be more receptive to you for the second date. What these are called: positive affirmations. When your thoughts are going off the tracks, bring them back on with positive reinforcement. One can remember in sports before the big play, a player will mutter to himself, "I got this." That is positive self-talk. Being your own personal Phil Jackson for all things life.

8. Not All Things in Life Are Black and White - Not everything is so clean cut and where one thing is perfectly good, and the other is wicked evil. If you don't get a perfect score on an algebra test doesn't mean you are not intelligent and deserve an F. Other more personal things, would be if you forget a friend's birthday, you are by default a horrible friend. That is just an extreme jump that one could just compartmentalize those thoughts as "made a mistake." Within this world, there are various shades of gray, and not all things are pitched back

and white, learn to block out the harshest extremes. Progress is about steady moves toward a lofty goal. Lots of time it takes incremental steps before you reach that Promised Land one wants.

9. Laughter Is the Best Medicine - Are your interests in life kind of on the dark side of things of horror and politics? Well, contrast that interest to tickle your funny bone. According to the National Library of Medicine, employees who had training based on humor helped reduce anxiety. There are other health benefits that studies have found, such as lowering depression and improving self-esteem and coping skills. According to the Mayo Clinic, it also stimulates organs, soothes tension, relieves pain, improves the immune system, improves mood, and helps personal satisfaction. If you are caught in the crossfire of the murky waters of life, start watching or listening to comedy to help tackle that Negative Voice in your head. One of the more interesting factoids: even if you are not in the laughing mood, you're not feeling it that day, imitating laughter can help lower your stress rate.

10. Make a Mental Note On Negative Thoughts - On July 23, 1993, in North Carolina, NBA Superstar Michael Jordan's father, James was killed in a robbery in an SUV. During his 'Above & Beyond' documentary of the 1995-1996 NBA season, Jordan talks about how his father taught him how to turn a negative into a positive. "It was a really difficult moment for me. Somehow, I kept my head high. I thought about all the things he used to tell me. Turn a negative into a positive. And here I was dealing with him in that way. It was tough." That same year he would win the MVP Award, the scoring title, the All-Star MVP, and the NBA Championship. What he did: he fought against negative thoughts and used them to fuel him. Once a

negative thought comes, don't lack it cripple your day but attempt to release it from your mind.

11. Reframe Negative Thoughts - If your negative thoughts are like a broken record, repeating and repeating and repeating, then learn to reframe them. From the Substance Abuse and Medical Health Services Administration, sponsored by the US. Department of Health & Human Services formulated this helpful guideline to augment negative thoughts with a positive twist. Building Self-Esteem: A Self-Help Guide (booklet SMA-3715) from them they devised this table of information:

Negative Thought
Positive Thought

I am not worth anything.
I am a valuable person.

I have never accomplished anything.
I have accomplished many things.

I always make mistakes.
I do many things well.

I am a jerk.
I am a great person.

I don't deserve a good life.
I deserve to be happy and healthy.

I am stupid.
I am smart.

12. Visual Images to Remove Dark Thoughts - There are many ways to get rid of that stew of negative thoughts. According to the National Library of Medicine, people with a mind that is keen on visual imagery tend to utilize it for memory performance. But not only that, using an image in your head that brings you calm, kitten, kangaroo, or that first kiss, is a good way to cleanse the mind of what nebulous thing that haunts your psyche. The other thing this can do: doesn't strengthen the imagination and the ability to retain information.

13. Zero in on What Exactly Is Giving Your Negative Thoughts - Chances are whatever you have in your mind that is negative, will make no difference in the outcome of what happens. And, chances are, it won't even happen. So localize what exactly is causing the negative thought, and look to compartmentalize it into the basements of your mind so it does not distract you. If you are feeling doomed and gloomy and have a big new job, recognize that those negative feelings will only hinder you from doing the job. Or if every time you go on a big road trip, you get nervous. But then remember each time you went on a road trip everything went fine and dandy. Whatever is bothering you, focus on it for a bit and realize it's counterproductive

14. Positive Energy Nonverbal Energy - Albert Mahrabian, an Armenian researcher, studied body language. His research found that fifty-five percent is nonverbal, thirty-eight percent is vocal, and seven percent is words. This means communicating positive energy and looking to surround yourself with people with equal positive energy for your own self-confidence. Simply communicating more positively, even with your body language, your gait, and your posture can help

take care of your glum spirit. Neurotransmitters like serotonin, endorphins, and dopamine, all positive meddles in the brain, can be activated by doing one simple thing: smile. See, when you smile, your mind releases molecules that are named neuropeptides. What these do: they can help ward off anxiety. It creates a ripple effect by both making you feel better and also helping you connect to people from that non-verbal signal. The moral of this story is if you got a frown, well.... try turning it upside down.

15. Blue - If your mind pitches black, then remember this: B.L.U.E. If after this you're still spiraling into negative thoughts there is one last tip. Ever wanted something simple, perhaps for a child or teenager, to remember to avoid self blame? Well, this is a psychology acronym standing for things to be mindful of.

B- Blaming myself;

L - Looking for the bad news;

U - Unhappy guessing;

E - Exaggeratedly negative.

3.2 Summary

These are some no-brainer trips to help improve a person's thought process. They can improve the positivity in your mind, accomplishments, and Self-Esteem. If you are a person caught in a real pitch-black place in life, and thinking of hurting yourself, or others, contact a counselor immediately, and you can turn your life around. In summary of this segment of this book, the key to turning off negative thoughts is catching them and then turning that into a positive one.

Chapter 4: Growth Mindsets Vs. Fixed Mindsets

Professor Carol Dweck was the psychologist who invented the term "Growth Mindset." Her study is about human motivation. She also won the APA Award for Distinguished Scientific Contributions to Psychology and thus knows a thing or two about just expanding your horizons in your psyche. What she did is found the distinguishing characteristics between a person with a growth mindset and those gridlocked in a fixed mindset. Psychologist Dr. Carol Dweck did various studies on high school students to pick their brains and understand the aforementioned mindsets. In a study just after Star Wars came out in 1978, she did two studies on 130 5th-grade children using a variety of difficulty-level puzzles. Some of the students embraced the difficulty and failure and thought of the harder puzzles as learning. They were optimistic. It's at this point that she put the phrase 'Growth mindset' on the psychology map.

This study ways in which a person with an open mind takes in information, cogitates in their cranium, and uses it for their self-improvement. Then there is the devil's advocate, the person that rejects it and believes people are just born with the ability and just stay stagnant and don't develop or… at a glacier's pace. It's really the question of nature versus nurture. These characteristics are established at a very young age and are both conscious and subconscious. But the truth of the matter is, growing is a lot of nurture. Simply being in a growth-mind frame it is believed you can increase your intelligence and talents using intense perseverance. But if you are in a fixed mindset, according to Dr. Dweck, those aspects cannot be developed. It's like four feet stuck in cement, and you can't move. Silence used to say the brain stops growing in adulthood, but in reality, the muscle in our skull never stops growing neurons. It's always changing its plasticity. But in terms of a growth mindset, to actually improve and grow skills one must have the tenacity to get the boldness of temerity. So here is a rudimentary breakdown of the difference between the two mindsets.

Growth Mindset - The name applies exactly what it is, but there is more to it than that. They know it will be a long row to hoe but they know perseverance is the key. It is a steadfast belief that your intelligence and skills improve with handwork. It's a willingness to take a calculating risk for self-improvement, where failure is possible. It's a belief that blood, sweat, and tears of handwork will lead to mastering skill. People within this frame of mind also look for role models to pattern their course of action after. The big thing: they see feedback as a way to improve and is crucial for their goals. They subscribe to the idea of lifelong learning. A growth mindset remains underfed to rejection but just keeps pressing on with optimism.

Fixed Mindset - These are people that see that talented people are just innately 'born' with ability. Their personalities see failure as catastrophic, they are shamed, they wallow in despair, and they give up easily if they don't have the whole deck in their favor. They like to sidestep challenges to avoid them. They see the success of other people and get a spark of jealousy and see them as threatening. The little feedback is like a personal vendetta against them. Their personalities give up easily with a pessimistic attitude.

Psychologist Dr. Carol Dweck also found some interesting other juicy nuggets of information: obviously, growth-minded kids had increased performance—-that's a no-brainer. Their minds are open; they know failure is a learning process and can re-strategize. She found that, in particular, kids in science and mathematics would especially have a marked improvement in grades. But they also found something else: people in a growth thinking pattern had reduced burnout, less depression, anxiety and psychological problems, and behavior problems. Meaning, for your livelihood, having a growth mindset for things called life is for your good. The University of Groningen created this helpful chart of what to watch for to get out of the shackles of Fix Mindset.

Situation
Fixed mindset approach
Growth mindset approach
You get a very high grade on an exam
Great! I must be really intelligent in this area
Great! I must have worked hard and learned a lot
You're starting a new assignment or project
I hope this will be easy for me
I hope this will be interesting!
You get negative feedback on your work
Oh no! This proves I'm no good at this
Okay, I need to get back to work and learn more

As the writer of the book, one has to naturally subscribe to the notion of a growth mindset. This profession requires a constant learning process, new words, new topics, new images, and a healthy dose of failure. That is the nature of what it is to be a writer. But that mindset is a good mindset to have for all professions.

There is the part of the book where you will expand your neuroplasticity and learn a bit about significant mumbo jumbo—bear with me, nonmedical people. The National Library of Medicine found Using Hypnotherapy and neuroimaging. These scientists measured that people with growth mindset brains are more active and have more focus on the process of doing it... rather than the end adult. They also found they are more apt to change course. All are key attitudes to development.

4.1 Steps How To Get Into a Growth Mindset:

A person can change their hard work and grit. Neuroscience reveals that your brain is malleable. It changes its plasticity through experiences and info. It also strengthens connections but in the same instant, grows new ones. It also reveals neurons are constantly growing in the brain. This means in layman's terms: you can change. So the million-dollar question is, how does one become a growth-minded person? Here are some basic principles to foster growth.

1. Determine What Your Mindset

Judging by the fact you purchased a book on growing your mind, chances are you are in a growth mindset. But if not, look inward, into your thoughts and maybe the pessimism you may have, and determine what you are, Fixed or Growth. As for your questions, how you could make calculating struggles to improve yourself. One of the other great benefits of being within a growth mindset is the ability to enter new fields through sheer will power and open-mindedness.

2. Understand 'Not Yet'

You are not a _____... yet. Think of the power in that three-letter word. How you could maybe get incredible failure from all angles, but if you simply tell yourself that you have a fighting chance for the next time around. It also rewires your mental pattern to see more of a long game at hand, not a short-term victory. The aforementioned pioneering psychologist in this mental framework, Dr. Dweck mentioned in her TED conference just how powerful the word Yet is. So if you have a series of hurdles, down on your luck, say to yourself not yet when you are looking to get your goals. It brings a degree of optimism that your goal is still within your grasp.

3. Take Pleasure in the Process

Whatever you're trying to do, if you learn to somehow converse with yourself to enjoy it then you have a better shot at improving at it. Simply learn to appreciate the handwork it takes, maybe the setbacks, and see the Growth Mindset journey as one Nintendo big game too, and things don't always work out your way. There is a saying, "it is not about the destination... it's about the journey.

4. Silence the Fix Mindset Voice

If you have the voice of George Costanza from Seinfeld in your head, that pessimistic attitude, learn to silence him. That negative Cognitive Distortions voice hinders your ability to have a growth mindset. This thinking pattern consumes a person with negativity and pessimism. Simply put: they are Hijacking Your Brain. There are a range of ways to fix this voice; hypnosis is one of them. Or just be mindful of that inner George Costanza in your head at all times. Say to yourself, "You can do this." Instead of "I can't do this." Even if it comes up short, it's a learning process, and you can try, try, and try again.

5. All Research Says You Can

As noted throughout this book, medical scientists used to think the brain could not grow, but then they learned quite the contrary. That is Scientific data proving that you can indeed develop your brain through neuroplasticity. The first chapter covers many techniques of ways to reinforce brain plasticity that same info works in spades for this area. Learn to get out of your comfort zone, that same beaten path. Challenge yourself to take control of your brain one day at a time.

6. Constructive Feedback

Whenever you produce something, be it a new sales technique, writing, Photoshop work, or an invented new Version of Astroturf, get some feedback on that. Listen to your peers, your parents, your customers, your clients, or whoever is there near you. Sometimes, people that are a bit too close to you may be skittish to offer the bluntest feedback you need. So seek a perfect stranger to what they think, and then do not get defensive… listen. Then re-strategize, if needed.

7. Get Out of Your Comfort Zone

This is a constantly repeated slogan on how to Change Your Mind. It's all about spearheading northward into untreated growth. If you don't like reading about medical science, it's hard to learn (for instance), well, learn about it, and maybe it can be informative. Not just with information but with how you move about the world. Instead of bike riding in loops around the park, venture onward into the city. It's a small thing like that, and repeating them, is how you grow and change your psyche for the betterment of your own good.

8. Make Mistakes

Part of getting out of your comfort zone is accepting mistakes will happen. But if you are in a growth-minded position, then you know that those mistakes are wondrous opportunities to learn and re-strategize. Nobody is perfect, and there have been a lot of mistakes and failures throughout history, but one thing is consistent failure can make you better if you learn to adjust course and learn. Be persistent and cultivate a Challenge.

9. Failure Is Part of the Growth Process

Academical ability isn't the only measuring stick of where you will go in life; it's also about handling failure correctly and steadfast perseverance. This is a memorable quote from legendary basketball player Micheal Jordan. "I've missed more than 9,000 shots in my career. I've lost almost 300 games. Twenty-six times I've been trusted to take the game-winning shot and miss. I've failed over and over and over again in my life. And that is why I succeed." It's the act of trying again and again, and perhaps failing again, that distinguishes the winners from the losers. See failure as deliberate practice for eventual success. You can be an F student and get the A life with just how you handle failure and what you do with it.

10. Be a Fan of Yourself

As narcissistic as it sounds, you gotta be your own buddy if you're gonna be venturing out into uncharted waters where rejection is possible. Having feelings of self-loathing is just going to exacerbate the obvious ups and downs that happen in life. Everybody has deficiencies and what is important is to be mindful of your positives. The world can be tough for you but do not also be tough on yourself too, which will only bring a negative voice in your head. Think of your positive attributes or your previous achievements to mitigate the melancholy feeling of failure. Be a fan of your work, if raw, see the positive part of it and also see the positive part of your own self. To have a growth mindset, try to develop a more optimistic disposition through all of life's obstacles.

11. Do Goldilock Tasks

These are things you could do that are not extremely difficult, and they are not easy peasy either. They are just outside of your familiar comfort zone, and they offer a challenge. That way, if you do it, you will not give up it will be a challenge but not exhausting. Find something that you can do that can expand your skill set for continuous improvement. Doing enough of these and never giving up can help shift your mindset to something that will promote meaningful growth.

12. Have Goals

If you are in a growth mindset, try to have some type of end game rather than just learning and expanding your horizons. The reason? It can be a strong motivation technique to spearhead you forward. Maybe, acquiring a certain score on some time of the test. Or, sales goal. Or maybe selling your first novel. Or, more realistically, getting a positive review from somebody. Then if you brainstorm a realistic, tangible goal, and visualize achieving that goal in your head, it helps it become more realized and possible. Just make sure and remember to set realistic goals and not to be a billionaire at 25 or give up on said Growth Mindset.

In closing, that is all the various steps for this segment. Being in the right frame of mind would also help develop entrepreneur skills where the completion is already re-strategizing and helps with resilience and keeping one grounded. Because in this thing called life, the pendulum swings different ways. A group of Fortune 1000 companies such as Apple, GE, Bloomberg, Microsoft, Uber, and Pinterest have all used their mindset for positive business growth. Here is some data from the study on why fostering growth is paramount for companies in the tech sector. This is what their data found:

- 47% more invested in their work
- 34% higher commitment to the company
- 47% more trust in the company
- 49% stronger belief that their company encourages innovation, which is essential to growth

These conglomerate companies like Apple and Microsoft have created a culture for limitless growth. Where calculated risks are good, and learning from failure is essential. Having a growth-minded approach to life gives you mental agility for innovation and is absolutely crucial for any budding entrepreneur. Professional Dweck remarked that focusing on people that are motivated by a challenge, working with people, and wanting to grow is more important than pedigree. If your company is within this thought pattern, it might be a good time for culture-shaping ignorer to gain a competitive advantage in the marketplace. Perhaps the greatest blunder by any company that uses the Fix mindset Vs. Growth mindset: It was Jan. 9, 2007, when Steve Jobs announced the first generation iPhone. It was a landmark device that changed, well, the whole world (for good or bad). It had a capacitive touch screen, a desktop-like web browser, an iPod, and a camera. It was the biggest break in tech since the personal computer. Even naysayers will have to admit that the iPhone changed the industry in one fell swoop.

But one thing to make a note of: the mindset differences between Microsoft's reaction and Google's reaction tectonic shift in the technology marketplace. At the time, they were knee-deep and working on their Android platform as something more similar to a BlackBerry with a keyboard they were looking to release soon. They had prototypes that were similar to Blackberry. But midway through Steve Jobs's meticulously planned presentation, they saw that was clearly the Next Generation of phones and the future.

Google saw the presentation and was floored. They scrapped their Blackberry knockoffs and went directly into making a phone like an iPhone. That was an example of a growth mindset. On the flip side, is Microsoft. They were at the time, the leader in the up-and-coming smartphone business. Microsoft CEO Steve Ballmer was dismissive of the iPhone. "Five hundred dollars? Fully subsidized? With a plan? I said that is the most expensive phone in the world." Then he said, "And it doesn't appeal to business customers because it doesn't have a keyboard. Which makes it not a very good email machine." Steve Ballmer said. Microsoft had the marketplace in an iron grip, and he was clearly in a fixed mindset. They were not looking to advance the phone to the next level but be complacent with their instantly dated Windows Mobile software... that blunder caused Microsoft to release their capacitive touch screen Windows phone years too late to the game. Meanwhile, because Google was in a growth mindset, they saw what the future held; they released Android within a year or iPhone's launch. Right now, Android and iPhone are neck and neck in market share in the US, with iPhone having a bit of advancement. Because Microsoft released too late and was in a fixed mindset, its platform never gained traction because it didn't have enough developer support. As Bill Gates said with software, "It's winner takes all."

This is why in business, it is crucial to be in a growth mindset and recognize the competition and not be dismissive of it.

4.2 Summary

As if you are a common person, not a multimillionaire tech guru, and just looking to get a leg up in life, these pillars for improvement to a growth mindset help you blossom. As with many things, if your chips are down, one has to go into a growth phase to get back on track. To fully comprehend all of the complexes of this, look into Carol Dweck's 2006 book, Mindset: The New Psychology of Success. Where she covered in intricate detail how she stumbled upon this discovery and gave additional information on how and can improve their mindsets on whether their chips are down or up in life. All of these elements are a cornerstone of self-improvement.

Chapter 5: How To Connect The Brain and Soul to Gain Mastery Over Emotional Intelligence

Aristotle wrote, "Some men . . . if they have first perceived and seen what is coming and have first roused themselves and their calculative faculty, are not defeated by their emotion, whether it be pleasant or painful." The key part to take out of that: is the defeat by their emotional part.

For centuries as far back as 350 B.C.E, Psychologists and philosophers thought cognition and emotion were separate. With the stand-fast idea that emotion hinders productivity. Like Mr. Spock in Star Trek, it is emotion versus sound logic. If you have emotion, you compromise yourself and your ability to think. But over time, psychologists learned they are in the same domain of understanding; they are interrelated and are essential for forming empathy and understanding oneself.

So what is EQ? In one sentence; it's the perception of your and others' emotions and then the ability to facilitate critical thinking. In three words: it's the management of emotions. Professional Thorndike in the Jazz era of the 1920s, coined the term social intelligence. It described it as, the "ability to understand and manage men and women, boys and girls, to act wisely in human relations." This history of the exact phase of Emotional Intelligence was pioneered in 1990, by John D. Mayer of UNH and Peter Salovey of Yale, two psychology professors. What their research paper covered was introducing the world to what is EQ. In simple terms, It is the ability to understand your emotions and others more efficiently. It is that cognition and emotion are connected, and one can discriminate a course of action from them. It is the ability to intricately understand people's emotional welfare used to mitigate stress, understand others and communicate, empathize with others, overcome difficult tasks and lessen conflict. Having a pinpoint understanding of emotions simply makes you a more efficient person.

An adequate understanding of EQ can help you with a range of things in life. Notwithstanding, successes in work and school, career, and building stronger connections with people by being more empathetic to their feelings. If you have the ability to understand not just your own emotions and intelligently change course, you can do the same with your interaction with people to be more efficient and shrewd decision-makers. The four pillars of EQ are the following:

Self-Management - It's to control your emotions, and saviors and manage your and others' feelings in positive ways. Using critical thinking skills to take initial emotional understanding, and the ability to adjust from understanding. It's to thoughtfully read emotions. This is also called self-perceived emotional intelligence (PEI).

Self-Awareness - It's to understand one's feelings and see how others detect those feelings you express. Understanding your own Achilles heel, your weakness, and having self-assurance upon understanding them.

Social Awareness - In social situations, it's to be a social butterfly and feel comfortable. You are empathetic and have concerns for people, and can pick up on social cues. You can see the power structure of groups and adjust accordingly.

Relationship Management - A team player who works well within a group and can mitigate conflict. Because of interpersonal skills, and empathy, you foster solid relationships. To each person, you are a good speaker, and because of that, you can inspire others.

Why Is EQ So Important?

Early man's common ancestor, Neanderthals, had to worry about hunting, finding shelter, and language skills were primitive at best. But thousands of years later, a crucial component is communication and understanding people. According to the National Library of Medicine, older adolescents, non-homeless people, and homeless older adolescents have similar IQs except for their verbal skills are slightly lesser. You can be an exemplary student but have poor social skills, and that could be your downfall by not understanding how vital EQ is. If that doesn't confine you, here are some other bullet points to inspire you. The other big thing to take out of this: according to research from the National Library of Medicine, EQ plays into happiness and lower EQ plays into being bullied in school.

Career/ Academic Performance

Your performance is interwoven with your understanding of people's emotions and how you can change accordingly. Prime example: interviews. EQ comes into play in that face-to-face meeting and many others where you are put under scrutiny by a stranger. If you have a firm grasp of sensibility to feelings, you can interact with people better and build bonds. Whenever you are hired for many jobs they have you do a computer test. What they are testing: your personality and emotional intelligence and how you interact with others. In the leadership position, a high Emotional intelligence correlates with organizational effectiveness.

Physical Health - Being plagued with stress and anxiety takes a toll on the heart and blood pressure, and immune system. Self-regulating emotions can help reading yourself and also learn how to de-escalate stressful situations. In addition, according to the National Library of Medicine, the lower the EQ, the higher the chances of phobias and self-harm. Critical thinking about your emotions and changing thought patterns can help you live longer. So whether you are in a high-stress personal situation, or dealing with an ill-tempered person, you could use EQ and look to decompress from the stress and preserve your own body....

Mental Health - Your mind and body work hand-in-hand. If you are a person that continuously spearheads into high-stress situations, when you can avoid them can get better results, that is where EQ could help. Having the skill set to reign in your worst impulses and thoughtfully communicate with people can help you from suffering from mental illnesses such as depression. Simply not interacting well with people can give you depression, and then you can spiral downward even more.

Relationship - People can come across as complex, no matter what their gender is. Having a firm understanding of understanding people's emotions, by it by their body language, minor social cues, fluctuations in voice or what they actually say, and anything in-between can help you foster relationships. Most of all, it helps you with your networking skills which are crucial for people in particular white-collar jobs, but it's also essential for anybody looking to methodically build connections. EQ plays highly in developing long-term relationships.

Social Intelligence - Having a precise understanding of your emotions and others helps in social situations. Company meetings, school interaction, team chemistry, all of it. Developing an understanding of social intelligence will help you understand who is one you can connect to, and not. Having a degree of intelligence of people's emotions in social gatherings can help you interact, lower stress and find love and prolong connections.

How To Develop Your EQ?

As Mahatma Gandhi once said, "Speak only if it improves upon the silence." If you want to develop your emotional intelligence, one has to begin to use critical thinking skills to understand your own emotions and others and then learn to change. Learn to defuse conflict situations and take out your stress on yourself. Understand your psyche and how emotion and judgment go hand and hand in each social interaction you have. Seek to build your social skills, perhaps listen more if you are a person who talks a lot, and learn to become empathetic with each encounter you have with a person. Listen to the rhythms of conversations, the body language, the tone of voice, the topics, and how you can interact with people more succinctly. Learn to be simpatico with other people.

Here are some things to look for to develop your EQ;

Self-regulation

Scenario: In a game of pick-up basketball, a player calls a foul that seems not to be a foul at all.
Higher EQ: You listen and agree with the foul in a way to see the bigger picture that it is just a pickup game of basketball. The relationship with the team is important.
Lower EQ: You get enraged and throw the basketball at the player and create an award situation for everybody on the court.

Empathy

Scenario; A girlfriend is not happy you forget her birthday and didn't even get her a card.

Higher EQ; You explain a legitimate why and apologize. You make up for it by doing something special for her.

Lower EQ: You brush it off, and do not understand why a woman must get a card on their birthday and don't understand their sensitivity for gift cards.

Self-Awareness

Scenario: You are at an off-hours company meeting, and there is a dress code.

Higher EQ: You wear exactly what you are supposed to wear and look to interact with others. You rarely do not use your phone.

Lower EQ: You wear something you are not supposed to, remain rebellious from the group, and play with your phone in a self-absorbed manner.

Motivation:

Scenario: You're looking to publish a book about Changing Your Mind.

High EQ: You tough through it, write a helpful book, and am grateful for anything that happens.

Lower EQ: You give up realizing writing a book is difficult and may not be a New York Times Best Seller.

Social Skills:

Scenario: You have a job interview tomorrow to be a software engineer at Apple.

High EQ: You make eye contact, firm handshake, answer questions well, and smile often.

Lower EQ: You do not make contact, have a weak handshake and answer questions non-efficiently and have a dour expression.

5.1 Steps How To Build Emotional Intelligence

1. Be Outgoing and Assertive

If you are a wallflower personality, try to be assertive and get out of your shell. Extend ourselves to make tangible connections to people. Instead of being the person standing in the corner, go into the group and talk. Start small, and work your way up. Practice understanding non-verbal cues and modulating your voice to show expression. Look to come out of your shell and harmonize with a group. Cultivate, creating more connections.

2. Handle Conflict With Ease

People with High-EQ know how to handle conflict. Sometimes it is just about keeping your voice mellow and your body language composed. Learn to handle each stressful encounter like a riddle you must solve the answer to. Understand sometimes you want a resolution, but other times it is best just to walk away knowing it's impossible to compromise with the person. Pick your battles wisely, and chances are unless it's a matter of life and death, no battle might be the best alternative.

3. Be A Expert Listener

"Change happens by listening and then starting a dialogue with the people who are doing something you don't believe is right." – Jane Goodall. Many people with Low-EQ only half-listen to what the other person says, wait for the person to stop talking, then talk. If one slows things down, and for a real rapport with the other and what they are saying, you can create a bond with them. Many people simply are not given full attention. Not only that, the person should take a greater liking to you if you listen with your ears open.

4. Be Motivated

People that have emotional intelligence firing on all cylinders, put forth a goal you could have to energize you throughout the day. Seek various goals you could have, not just one. Sometimes growth comes from increments, ups, and downs, but one must look at the bigger picture to see progress. Use emotional intelligence to understand your emotions when things are not working your way.

5. Practice Having a Positive Frame of Mind

If you have a positive attitude when interacting with people, be it smile, topic, or body language it can be infectious to draw people towards you. Merely having a positive outlook helps you harness connections and develop even more positive growth. Having an understanding that your body language is more than half of your communication with people... and a lot of people can see if you are on the positive or negative spectrum by your body language. Keep a sunny-side optimistic spirit at all times. The glass IS half full, remember.

6. Self Awareness

. Emotionally intelligent people know of the vibe they are giving off and can change it. If you are having a bad day, be self-aware to try not to project that, be cheerful, or you will push people away from you. Everybody has a bad day, but how you handle it is the difference between Low-EQ and High-EQ. If you realize you are going 'out of the pocket,' go right back in to help foster connections and mitigate alienation. Have an awareness of one's faults and seek to correct them using practices.

7. Handle Feedback With Grace

Everybody (probably) has gotten a score they wish they have never gotten. It hurt. Maybe it drags your day down into the dumpster. But how you handle it says a lot about your personality. Lebron James lost in the NBA Finals twice before we won an NBA Championship. He also had a series of setbacks in other series. What he did is he got better and listened to the criticism from the media that he wasn't assertive enough and needed to develop a low-post game. Through measured strides, and listening, he got better So even the greats are criticized. Success in life comes from how you tackle failure.

8. Look To Understand People's Feelings.

Each person has a different story, and many people are full of hardships, and maybe people never know. If you see a person angry for trivial things, there is probably a reason why in their personal life. Look to see people as books that one could empathize with, even if they are very different from you. Look to read people's feelings using EQ and share common ground to help create bonds. If you find a self-absorbed person, try to find out why. Or Vice versa.

9. Develop Leadership Skills

Leaders have a certain panache about them. They take charge. They are insertive. They listen. They have humor. Their personalities are bold. That is the skillset one should look to develop to fully utilize emotional intelligence training. If you are a reserved person who it's too absorbed in the computer, realize it's gonna take probably years to develop that skill. But the path begins with one first step.

10. Understand The Power of First Impressions

How you are dressed, how you communicate, and your facial features are all some of the first impressions that people get from you. Learn to be approachable and learn how to disarm people if you may come across as intimidating. Have an understanding that nonverbal communication is over half of communication and many people are kind of shy, especially in certain fields. Learn to have people drawn to you by a sense of humor and cheek to cheek smile.

5.2 Summary

All of these are many skills that can help you build the foundations of changing your mind and also developing a high emotional intelligence. As noted, you're not exactly gonna be a social butterfly and have a mastery of emotional intelligence overnight. To be blunt, it may take years for you to fully come out of your shell if you're a person who struggles with self-confidence. But with determination, understanding of human psychology, continuous motivation, and utilizing the teachings of emotional intelligence... you could be well on your way.

Chapter 6: Natural Brain Detoxes and How Sleep Is a Key Component of Learning

There is lifespan, and then there is brainpan. Which means, how long your brain can stay in peak homeostasis performance. The following information on how vital sleep is to peak mental health—-and perhaps the most important chapter in the whole book on brain health. This is the part of the book where the author will dry to avoid quick remedies and wonder drugs. The primary reason is your liver and kidney, and a little thing called sleep care or detoxification. Within your brain is the glymphatic system, and the rest of the body's system is called the lymphatic, minus the G. Glymphatic was only named in 2013 as the central nervous system (CNS) of vertebrates, a way of removing waste. The term glymphatic system was invented by Maiken Nedergaard, a Danish neuroscientist. Without getting overly medical here with too much neuroscience mumbo-jumbo, this helps reduce soluble proteins and metabolites and waste to your body on these things called (big word) perivascular channels. The brain must be within a form of the cavity (sleep works too) to remove potentially neurotoxic waste from the mind for homeostasis (healthy brain). It helps the brain cleanse parenchymal tissue (covering). Chances are, this info is a lot to take in, but it's not as difficult as it sounds. The brain is a muscle with fluids and blood flow and needs to be restored. Which transitions to the topic of the chapter: detoxification. Other things, what you look for your when the brain needs detox Some of the issues when your brain is overworked is problems with brain fog (A "Long Covid" symptom), fatigue, and memory loss, (All common issue with people who had Covid-19) depression, head injury, stroke, addiction, and nerve-wracking anxiety. If your brain has all of these caveats going on, it's time to detox, pronto First, except for stroke, this is the logical solution to no-pills, no-frills restorative treatment of your brain. What more motivation? Having an understanding of this and taking action can reduce the likelihood of neurodegenerative diseases like Alzheimer's. One other thing, when we sleep, we increase glymphatic activity to remove more waste from our brain. The first thing on the oodles of steps to help promote detoxification of your is a little thing called meaningful restorative sleep.

6.1 Ways to Detox The Brain

1. Sleep

There have been endless studies on just how crucial sleep is to the brain. One of the biggest things it does is not just feeling refreshed to tackle your day, but to your overall physical and mental prowess and most of all, removing toxic molecules and also the removal of unwanted proteins. This is according to Dr. Phyllis Zee, a professor of neurology at Northwestern University Feinberg School of Medicine. The average person sleeps 6.5 hours per night, yet the National Sleep Foundation says healthy adults need 7-9 hours per night. That gap between the two affects the ability to learn. Dr. Matthew Walker, Neuroscientist and Psychology at the University, and also the Founder and Director of the Center for Human Sleep of California, goes into detail about how crucial sleep is to your brain and overall health. For the hippocampus to properly encode learning and memories, you need seven to nine hours of sleep. It has been researched less than optimal sleep decreases learning by 40 percent. Sleep is, quite simply, a 'Save Button' for memory. What various studies have learned is REM sleep helps you embed information that you learned into your brain. Deep Sleep, according to Dr. Walker, is about gathering your knowledge together. But REM sleep is about processing it subconsciously to engrain memory into the neural architecture of the brain. Just to belabor the point, There is a saying, "Sleep on it." But that saying has scientific data saying that is, in fact, true. If you have a problem, you can have dream-inspired insight into how to solve the problem. Dmitri Mendeleev, an early 18th-century Russian chemist, invented the periodic table of elements, a way to display chemical elements (Li, Cs, Ac, etc.) from dream inspiration. Auto Loi won the Nobel Peace Prize through chemical transpiration through nerve cells from dream inspiration. Probably the most widely known story of dream inspiration is when Paul McCartney dreamed of the melody to the song Yesterday. Each of those examples was men who used sleep for problem-solving and little creativity. However, it is more likely, your brain will be more mentally engrossed in solving the problem in the morning, not by any epiphany like a dream like a Beatle but more just from getting proper rest—it is crucial to brain health and retaining information. Just like clicking Command + S on your keyboard to save a Word document—that's why slumber does. How to respect to retain the information you learn, much less from this book, if your brain is too exhausted to retain it?

Example: Integration of relational memory testing. According to a study posted on Springer (a leading global scientific publisher on topics of Cognitive, Affective, & Behavioral Neuroscience) in 2011, they reported that sleep helps you retain your memory but also catalogs "relational memories." During an experiment, people were tested on the impact of insomnia on the cognitive thinking of the brain. (Ellenbogen et al., 2007, as cited in Walker, 2009). During this, people were taught 5 paired associates, relational pairs, and direct associates of letters. They are called premise pairs of the following A>B, B>C, C>D, and D>E. The group was not told of the overreaching hierarchy, and they were put into 3 groups. The group that slept in-between had 25% retaining the information. Sleep is key in decision-making.

Furthermore, there are lingering effects of not getting enough sleep, such as the massive drop in Natural Kills Cells and your overall body's immune system and warding off mental illnesses like Alzheimer's, cancers, preventing diabetes, regulation of blood sugar, joints, and a healthy heart. In the most simple terms of the common tongue, Everything is tied to sleep and managing a healthy circadian rhythm and healthy sleep routine. So, if you want to boost your brain and retain the information you learned today and within this book? Sleep 7-9 hours a night.

2. Quality Anti-Inflammatory Foods

There is a saying, "we are what we eat." Another one is, " We are what we consume." You get the point. What you put into your body, be it the overzealous amount of processed food or a healthy Mediterranean diet of fish, vegetables, and fruits, each plays a critical rule in your cognitive performance and synapse and connections in your brain. Also, just like the above topic, it ties into how well your organs work and also helps with focus, lowering depression and anxiety and boosting free radicals and antioxidants for peak body function. These are some recommendations to consume to not just help your physiological and psychological functions:

- The Mediterranean diet
- Fruits
- Vegetables
- Fish
- Shellfish
- Seaweed
- Seeds
- Yogurts
- Herbs
- Spices

- Tarmac
- Talic
- Rosemary
- Yogurts and other probiotic foods
- Nuts and seeds
- Honey
- Legumes and beans
- Chocolate
- Tea
- Coffee

In terms of that last one, Coffee is a psychoactive stimulant. According to the National Library of Medicine, coffee increases the body's energy metabolism within the brain and reduces blood flow from hypoperfusion and something called noradrenaline for the fight-or-flight response. It energizes you and also makes you happier through a hormonal chemical called dopamine. So coffee makes you feel good and also makes your brain sharper—-but use it in moderation. The sleep segment goes into the dangers of insomnia. But one thing people do not realize: according to sleep research, 25% of the caffeine in coffee is still in your body 12 hours later. This means coffee will get you sharper, but it says in the body for so long it will affect the quality of your sleep. So be mindful when using it and make sure you are fully rested in the morning, revitalized, or cut back on consumption of this psychoactive stimulant. How powerful coffee is in terms of varies by individual sensitivity? In terms of going into more detail, there are tons of books to learn about eating a proper diet. The best is to try to stick to more of the Mediterranean diet, more fish, more nuts, more vegetables and fruit. Look for food with anti-inflammatory, antioxidant, and anti-carcinogenic effects to help assist your brain. Finally, try to eat simple sustenance from products of Mother Earth and not from a factory. (Drugs and heavy alcoholic drinks are still and) For example, stuff without five or six-syllable words in the nutritional facts. So these are just some basics, and one can assume all adults know what quality food is and what is processed junk. But what you put into your body helps your brain and promotes vascular health.

3. Be Aware of Technology Addiction

Your way of being aware of your surroundings comes from early man and his desire to be aware of his surroundings in the grass savannah or the jungle. It is called the fight-or-flight response. Their body releases this hormone called cortisol to keep them hyper-aware, so they are eaten by a marauding pack of lions and scavenge for food off the bone and shelter. Flash forward 2 million years to the rise of the addictive properties of the Smartphone. Whenever you put your phone down, the adrenal gland in the brain releases that same cortisol that is tied to that flight or flight response. It is documented that we check out the phone every 15 minutes throughout the day. When you don't check your phone, your brain develops cortisol, and it starts to make you anxious like a lurking predator is on the attack or your body needs food. Rather than using that flight or flight response to attack, hunt and run, it's being used to keep you addicted by way of understanding the brain like a neurogenesis scientist.

Silicon Valley is basically brain-hacking people to become addicted to social media. They use algorithms and are finally adept at reading every keyword that you approve of to sell your advertisement but in addition, curating your content gets you consistently more addicted. On phones nowadays, there are activity monitors to restrict how much you are using them, which could benefit your brain from being distracted with addictive nonsense all day. There is a 60 Minutes episode from April 2017 with a Google developer where he gives insight into a system that is hijacking people's attention. He compares it to having a slot machine in your hand, a "Race to the bottom of the brainstem." and you keep using it no matter how unhealthy it is to your psyche. So if you see yourself constantly scrolling Instagram, Twitter, or Facebook, half a self-awareness to that cortisol release, shut it off and do something more rejuvenating to your brain.

4. Appreciate the Greater Outdoors

This is a great way to remove the toxicity of a frazzled web of emotions out of your brain… casual nature walks. Almost forty people were put in a scientific study to determine the health benefits of nature and external factors For 50 minutes. According to the National Library of Medicine, walking improves your condition, relieves stress, and also increases gratitude to detox your mind.

Simply taking a 10 to 20-minute walking brain through a forest, near a lake, or beach can help you foster new ideas and creativity but also simply clean your mind of whatever stress you may have lurking in the background. It is also noted that employers that have met in great outdoors have employees more engaged with positive rapport with one another, and it cuts down on the internal brick-and-mortar distractions of copy machines, cooks, or whatever misc sounds that may come into play in an indoor meeting. There are various reasons why you should be taking a brief time outside to detox your brain. On an additional note, if you own a dog…you are forced to go on scenic walks, and that may be something to consider.

5. Expand Real Life Social Network

In the age of Internet social networks, everybody's building friendships through that method, especially the younger crowd.

But building real connections to people or you could see personally doing activities is a good way to relieve the toxicity out of your brain and naturally relieve stress and is intrinsic to happiness. If you are miserable and things are going well, this is the logical first step to bring your emotions into more of a positive mindset in your friendship with people. If you are down in the dumps, depressing and full of whirlwind toxic thoughts and little connection to a not spoken friend in a while can help detoxify your brain. A University of Chicago researcher did a study on people talking to strangers on buses, strangers or being mute. Well, talking to strangers is... better than talking to nobody and will help bring a crucial dopamine release. So if you are a lone wolf, or maybe a social butterfly, expanding your network of friends—positive friends, can help detoxify your brain and bring about homeostasis (good mine) and work that glymphatic system in your mind for brain health.

6. Reduce Toxin Exposure

Like a lurking leviathan in the deep, there are chemicals all over lurking beyond just household products. It's Everywhere. Make a calculating effort to consume more organic products. Avoid plastics, pesticides (wash food), carcinogen-laced weed killers, beauty products, and cleaning products. Stop using plastic bottles and look for "BPA-Free" labeling. Wash hands often. Make a calculating attempt to mitigate the consumption of toxicity in your life. Use a vacuum with a HEPA filter. The water filter company Brita, has made excellent filters to either put on your tap directly or pour pitcher to help remove toxicity in the water. Another tip, in order to mitigate pesticides from the grass on the bottom of your shoe, take them off when you come into your house. These are various techniques to curtail your body from consuming unnecessary toxic exposure throughout the world.

7. Exercise But Also Stay Hydrated

Last but not least, is the no-brainer to detoxing. This topic is covered above so one doesn't need to belabor the point of the importance of exercises. But to improve your brain, increase waste clearance by way of glymphatic activity and have peak cardiovascular health. But the other thing is keeping yourself hydrated to the good value of lymphatic (non-brain) and glymphatic (brain) acuity in your body. It's also crucial to memory and learning and will help you reduce neurological disorders like Alzheimer's or Parkinson's and have more energy through the day to tackle more work.

6.2 Summary:

The single best way to detox your brain is to eat right, avoid substances, and most importantly, sleep 7-9 hours per night. After you are reading this book, it's highly advised to watch the Ted Conference by renowned UC Berkeley psychologist and sleep Guru Professor Matt Walker. He gives astonishing insight to just how extraordinarily important your sleep is to the entirety of your health. As he says in his video conferences, sleep is truly your superpower, and it also is the first thing in the morning that will spearhead you forward to changing your mind.

Chapter 7: A List of Advanced Mindfulness and Meditation Techniques

Eastern traditions have practiced meditation for thousands of years. From Chinese Qigong meditation. To The Japanese "Zen." Or the Indian Dhyana form. This book will cover the Indian form and term. The word 'meditation' derives from practices to focus the mind and body together, in a way to bring inner peace and well-being. Some practices are about sensation, others breathing, or sound, an image that is held in the mind. Another form is a mantra, is a rebated prose or word which is the signature part of what is called transcendental meditation.

The Guru of T.M. was Maharishi Mahesh Yogi, who was a global meditation teacher in Jabalpur, India. In 1959, he traveled around the world to teach meditation. For some mediation is kind of shrouded in mystery as the equivalence of religion or whatnot. Rather is just teaching about relaxation and focusing. His teachings are taught all over the world. A prime example of Mindfulness-based meditation would be in the late flower power era of the 1960s, The Beatles met him in Rishikesh, India, and some of their greatest work was inspired by the trip—-including lots of The White Album was written there. The Quiet Beatle, George Harrison, was in particular captivated by him after his many years of interest in meditation—-perhaps as a way to cope with the pressure and anxiety of being in a world-famous band when his personality was more reserved. The teaching was to practice inner calmness and enlightenment. This means these ancient teachings could help one develop a new idea they never thought they'd tap into.

Maharishi, now deceased in 2008, was a man who practiced Transcendental Meditation. If you put the name The Beatles and then some Indian spiritual teacher with a long usual name, you may think this is some pretty outlandish stuff going on. But it is reality... it's just about practicing a peaceful mind with things that are stressing you out. There are various ways to do meditation, some are slightly more complex, but for a beginner, just practicing the very basics of just mindfulness—-which is just a term for focusing your attention on something without being distracted. That is something that comes into play with learning but also relaxation to cope with the abundance of stress and distractions in life. Though this will avoid some of the more religious-sounding stuff, that can be found in his 1994 book Maharishi Vedic University, which may or may not be your cup of tea. For accessible sake, we will just keep this to the bare essentials that anybody can do. The practice calms you and in the same breath, will help you learn and focus. The practices help to just get rid of stress and how to develop a greater focus on whatever they want to do in life. Here are some benefactions of meditation:

Improves Inner Peace And Psychical Health -- There is a laundry list of reasons why one should practice meditation. First and foremost, it can improve your happiness. It simply makes it so you are attuned with the world and find more solace in simple pleasures. It takes the stresses of the whole world down a couple of notches, and you can find more pleasure in casual activities. It also helps you deal with conflict, and when you get a bad hand in cards in life, things in life are not working in your favor.

As the mind and the body are connected, and because of that thing built into us called the Flight-And-Fight response, your psychic health can improve too. Once you can convince yourself that giving a less-than-perfect score on something isn't exactly like having a teeming band of lions chasing you in the forest, then your old body relaxes, and you can lower your blood pressure, which will have to reduce pain and make your sleep better and improve gastrointestinal difficulties. The mind and the body connect, and simply finding peace in your mind when your chips are down, you can improve your body. Other things mindful is said to improve:

- Improve cognition
- Improves concentration
- Improves memory
- Improves resultants
- Antidote for stress
- Lowers fatigue
- Lowers anxiety
- Lowers symptoms of asthma in kids and adolescents
- Lowers hypertension
- Lowers aggressive disposition of males
- Lowers migraine symptoms

NOTE: According to the National Institutes of Health, the scientific studies on this have not been rigorous— but from this author's perspective: it will help you relax and sleep. Knowing the above chapter's scientifically proven data of how important sleep is to one's personal health to avoid degenerative diseases is reason enough to do it.

However, according to a Harvard study, some actual scientific data proves that it does help relieve depression. 16.1 million Americans in 2015 reported having signs of depression in the last 365 days. Massachusetts General Hospital did a study on mediation on the bay using MRIs on the brain to see the changes over eight eights of mindfulness in a 'stress reduction course/" What they found is when examining the brain using an MRI. They focused on the amygdala of the brain, which is an almond-shaped cluster of cells. It also is the fearful and threatening stimuli. It also controls the brain's emotions, and especially fear-related snap judgment made decisions. Researchers saw after eight weeks the people's amygdala was 'less activated' after mindfulness. Which is the raw data: you want to relax your amygdala, and practice meditation.

7. 1 The Data On How Widely Used Is Meditation

From a 2017 study, the number of people that did any form of meditation, from mantra or mindfulness, tripled in the five years starting in 2012. It increased from 4.1 of Americans to 14.2 percent. That's a staggering increase of people more interested in releasing tension from one's life. Over the years, meditative schools are becoming popular. In the same study, 1.9 percent of 34,525 people reported they practiced mindfulness in the last year. Among others who did mindfulness, 73% did it for their overall health and to prevent diseases. The biggest number, 93%, said they did it just to mitigate stress. Half of the ones surfed, it was to sleep better at night. The other thing to take into account, smartphone growth has made mediation extremely simple. One, in particular, an app named CALM, is a meditation and breathing app that has four million subscribers. In 2017, Apple awarded Calm the App-of-the-Year of award. So this practice is becoming extremely more mainstream thanks to the influx of technology and meditation schooling.

There are many different styles of meditation and transcendental meditation. But here is a basic meditation form of Yoga of just relaxing. This is called Anapanasati or by the common tongue "Meditation breathing." Let's begin with something simple that doesn't use any mantra and is just about breathing.

7.2 Steps for Different Types of Meditation

Beginner Meditation Breathe

1. Find a Quiet Place and Get Comfortable

Located in a quiet place with no distractions. No dogs. No cats. Or children. Just you and your peace of mind. For a more modern twist to this, you get mediation apps in App Stores. The author recommends Calm, which has various styles and also calm and soothing (and intentionally boring) sleep stories for people with episodes of insomnia. Another one cuts down on non-controllable noise within or outside your bedroom, you could find noise-canceling headphones or high-end earbuds like AirPod Pro. By way of the newer technology called Noise-Canceling, many newer ones can cancel out virtually all sound and can be a revelation for people who want calm.

2. Sit Down Somewhere

For some people or nimble, you could be cross-legged but for people not, just sit straight with good posture. You could do this even in an office chair. though some like to meditate laying down somewhere. Whatever you prefer.

3. Relax Your Mind

Calm your mind and clear your mind of distractions. Then close your eyes and set a timer for 5 minutes. Clear your mind of worries and start taking a few deep but natural breaths through your nose and then through your mouth. However, it's not any icon-clad rule; breathe what feels comfortable. Then let the breath be felt through your stomach and do this for 5 minutes.

4. Focus On Your Breathing

Focus on how you are breathing and how it feels when you inhale and exhale. What that does is it blocks your consciousness from focusing on stressful things or distractions. Think of joy around you and inner peace to lower your blood pressure and just help you decompress for five minutes.

5. Refocus Thoughts

When first doing this, or when in a high-stress period in life, it can be challenging to just think of little to nothing. But focusing on your breath, or something on your body that might be tingling or whatnot will remove the cleansing of your thoughts. Rather like how some of the chapters bring up ways to cleanse your brain through sleep, and food, this cleans out your concourses of nagging the trifle of worries and stress you may have.

6. Put In The Work to Practice Often

Like many things in life, it may take a bit of time to get good at it. Michael Jordan didn't make the high school basketball team on the first try, and meditation takes a bit of practice too. But this is pretty entry-level mediation to just find a quiet place and just compress. There are various smart watches and whatnot, Apple Watch, that can ding you when your heart rate is unusually high, and then you can practice a breathing technique within an app. Just be vigilant to do some type of reacting station techniques to help lower blood pressure, sleep better (crucial), decrease stress, and help you regain focus on whatever you want to accomplish in life.

Intermediate "4-7-8 Breathing Technique".

This is another stress antidote. However, the breathing style is slightly (really) more complex as it requires counting, which is the main distinguishing factor from the aforementioned. Other than that, it's the same thing. Some doctors recommend doing this twice a day, but if that is too much, try a good quiet time to do it around mid-day when things are most stressful. Essentially, you do the same thing as above, except with this

- Inhale and breathe within your nose for two seconds
- Hold your breath for 3 seconds
- Release your breath through your nose for 4 seconds with a whoosh sound

Do this for five minutes. The exact second count is not that big of a deal, just stick to a count and use the above as a guide. If you have difficulty holding your breath, just do what feels most relaxing. It's that simple.

Advanced (Slightly More) "Universe" Meditation

This is a practice that is more advanced than the Maharishi Mahesh Yogi realm and involves a 'mantra' or, in simple terms, a repeated phrase. Sometimes when you meditate, you have to mix it up a little bit, or you become less focused to be mindful. It also might not be many people's cup of tea. But within a growth mindset, taught in this book, it could be open to different things, and learning about consciousness is just another feather in one's cap of learning. This is about shifting yourself to being "in the universe" and then having the thought of "the universe being in us."

1. Find a Quiet Place and Get Comfortable

Just like the previous, you do the same thing. Find a place, inside your house, outside in a park, where you can sit, and it's quiet.

2. Sit Down Somewhere

The same thing, sit down. Cross-legged if you can. If you are less flexible or very tall, just sit somewhere comfortable (lay down)

3. Relax, Imagine And Whisper

Form a blockade in your psyche for negative thoughts and close your eyes. Then repeat this stuff to yourself in a whisper, "I am not in the mind, the mine is in me." Then imagine a bubble of your expanding consciousness that covers your head. Feel it grow within you and repeat that.

Imagine this bubble over your body and then repeat in a whisper, "I am not in the body, the body is in me."
Then repeat, "I am not in this room, the room is in me."
As your consciousness figuratively expands around the building mutter,

"I am not in this building, the building is me."
It's here where I think you may have a point.
"I am not in this city, the city is in me."
Then.
"I am not in this country, the country is in me."
Then.
"I am not in this world, this world is in me."
Then,
"I am not in this universe, this universe is with me."

As one can see, which originally sounded kind of New Age and far-fetched Indian Mediation, one can kind of get an understanding of what this is doing: it takes your mind out of your current trials and tribulations of life to de-stress and take your mind elsewhere—even the outer cosmo and the furthest reaches of the known or unknown galaxy.

7. 3 Summary:

Meditation has its roots in Buddhism, but you don't need to have a budget to do it. Even such athletes as LeBron James have been known to do it during the sidelights to develop inner peace and get a sense of calm. Anybody can do it, and with a laundry list of apps available in smartphone app stores, it's easier than ever to simply learn how to create a sense of tranquility in the psyche to help mitigate all the stresses of this thing called life. Meditation can be utterly transformative to have a person have not just a different outlook in life but also simply feel mentally restored like they never have before.

Chapter 8: Formulating a Strategy

The 17th-century French Military mastermind Napoléon Bonaparte knew a thing or two about strategy. So brazenly inventive were the strategies that he pioneered in how the war was done. His enemies were playing checkers, and he was playing chess. Example: During the European Napoleonic Wars, in his quest to conquer Europe, he would use a diversionary tactic to attack the enemy on its flanks instead of attacking them head-on, to avoid the line of cannon. Meaning a blindside and then baffling them with an unorthodox strategy. He also would order his military to lure the enemy onto thin ice, encircle them, and then use cannons to destroy the ice as they fell into it. He would study up on Alexander The Great, Hannibal Barca, Julius Caesar, Gustavus Adolphus, Henri Turenne, and Frederic the Great and formulate the best methods of victory on the battlefield. Though he would get a little foolhardy and invade Russia, and after he sent in 600,000 soldiers—only 100,000 would return. He would later be imprisoned, convicted, and exiled from his country and marooned on an island when he had the world at his fingertips of his innovative strategies. However, he has his run of being a brilliant military mind, the likes of which nobody had seen. He was one of the most famous—-if not the most—skilled military tacticians in all of history. These are some good techniques that can help you succeed: but confidence and erratic behavior can lead you to your doom. The bases covered in this book on topics of expanding the mind through neuroplasticity, sleeping well, eating well, and doing all of the aforementioned things will only do so much without actually formulating a worthwhile strategy. You gotta follow through. Not just take in—-but do.

One could take an educated guess that many people reading this book are bringing about a new career strategy. This brings up an important aspect of How To Change Your Mind, strategic planning. These are skill sets that are some of the most coveted skills you can have in the job marketplace. Being a person who has critical thinking skills, and can process things logically is exactly what companies want for somebody in a management position.

So What Are Strategic Thinking Skills?

You know the basics of what this is; you are an adult. To know the finest details of this takes a bit more learning. What this can do, of course, is be able to solve complex problems, plan, and all the basics of things that they are aforementioned Napoleon did to a T. But there are outlines and definitions of exact kinds of strategic thinking. Knowing these helps one think even better in a strategic manner.

Analytical Skills - Formulating information through observation and study.

Communication Skills - Speak to people with a clear vision, and network with people who can help you support your strategy.
Problem-Solving-Skills - When the Jigsaw puzzle has many pieces, you can solve the puzzle.
Planning Skills - The ability to put forth a coherent strategy that is tethered to reality.
Management Skills - The ability to lead, inspire and guide people to further your mission and also keep people in a positive frame of mind.

With the basics of what is strategic thinking out of the way, let's get into the nitty-gritty of things that can inspire you, your workforce, or your just common everyday desire for self-improvement. Developing these skills requires the initiative to do it, a growth mindset, but also putting in the grit to do it and practice it throughout life and business.

8.1 Ways to Formulating a Strategy

1. Start With a Clear Vision

A good idea can go a long way to materialize into reality. If your ambition is to be the next Oprah Winfrey, study up on her biography and how she came to prominence. First, she worked at Baltimore's WJZ-TV as a news anchor. She used that platform to catapult her to daytime TV shows which he later used as an essential vehicle to promote her various businesses. Though all the pieces came to gather, she had a vision of what she wanted to do with her business empire with a brand for the betterment of America's women. She had a purpose of delivering goodness. From books to diets, to mentally therapeutic shows, he had the plan to deliver goodness to her audience and make them feel better with tips and insight into the human condition. It's unclear if this came together as a devised strategy from the get-go Baltimore's WJZ-TV (unlucky), or if she just stumbled into it (likely), but it worked because she had a visionary belief herself to become the world's first African American woman billionaire. One thing you can say: she did really work hard, and it was no fluke. He was a uniquely informed woman with great ambition and anybody who strikes it big, some good luck came her way.

2. Look At Strengths and Weaknesses

Conventional wisdom is whatever your current situation is, examine your predicament and study your weaknesses. Some people have a natural proclivity toward creative endeavors. Other people are more structured, disciplined, and mathematical. Everybody has weaknesses, and learning how to play to your strengths can be the difference between success and failure.

When you can devise a strategy that plays off your most positive attributes and meditates on your weaknesses, you can have a better avenue for success. If you are a person who is weak in one era, learn to develop that bit by bit, and that could one day be your strength as a person. Formulate a way to press onward using your best ability and then incrementally and steadily improve your weaknesses. This is what all great strategy technicians play.

3. Study Trends That Can Be Utilized

Beware of the necessity of strategic transformation. Before the iPhone came out, smartphones had been around for years. In 1992, the Simon Personal Communicator was released. Which were a phone with a keyboard and a monochrome album touchscreen. Smartphones with a keyboard were trending upward each year with web browsers and simple apps. As you may guess, you can see what happened. In the early 2000s, Blackberry started to take off with a text messaging keyboard. Apple studied the marketplace and brought forth its own spin on the smartphone and brought back a more polished and multi-touch screen. They study trends and combine their various strengths in the iPad sector and Computer to create a revolutionary (but flawed first-generation) product. What one can do from this, is study steadily rising trends and see if one can bring forth something new to the equation. By it, writing a book in a popular genre where other genres are less popular (Zombie genre in a post-pandemic world, for instance) or something simple like selling shirts (like putting something on the shirt that is 'trending'). Find something that is 'catching on' and inspires you in creating or in business directions. There are ideas all over; one has to have an open mind to think about them for a surefooted strategy.

4. Communicate Goals

If you run a business, communicate to your employees better about your goals. The reason: From Harvard Business Review, 95% of employees they work for don't understand their company's strategy. The same research says that 85% of leaders spend less than one hour per month conveying what their strategy is. That leads to confusion in the company's workforce to get everybody on the same boat. If you have people around you in a similar field, communicate with them about some of your goals. One doesn't have to be any big level of ownership to communicate better too. Simply find peers and talk to them about some of your goals, and maybe you can formulate new ideas from some of the dialogue you are having with them of how you can expand your horizons to a new frontier.

5. Growth Arc and Decline

Microsoft didn't become the market leader for market share overnight. Bill Gates saw a strategy of selling Software to fenders and then using a licensing fee. Year by year, they began to take over the marketplace, and by the early 90s, with Windows 95, it was total domination. They had a strategy that cemented that lead. From Microsoft's inception on April 4, 1975, in Albuquerque, New Mexico as a tiny company, to becoming the world's richest man in 1995, it took time. On the flip side, as Apple was on the verge of bankruptcy in the 90s, they slowly crawled back with the release of the iMac, and the iPod and then changed the world with the iPhone, and then July 31, 2020, Apple became the world's biggest company. The two companies along with Saudi Aramco are neck and neck for who will be the biggest company in the world. The other thing to keep in mind, if you are starting a company, is realizing the 'peak' and then knowing most companies grandparents grew up on have diminished or are gone. In the year 1961, the top 25 companies on the Fortune 500 in 1961, there are only 6 still around. So be watchful of your company's steady rise to a peak and then becoming lackadaisical, ignoring the above market trends, and then declining and slowly diminishing.

6. Re-strategy When Needed

Throughout this book, there is a mention of a 'growth mindset,' and one must apply those to a strategy. Once you rest on your laurels, that is when you and your company go from peak to decline. Strategic planning is continuous as the market and, well, the whole world is always changing. A good example is RKO Pictures. They produced many classic movies of Hollywood's Golden Age. Including King Kong, Citizen Kane, It's a Wonderful Life, Snow White, and the Seven Dwarfs. RKO was one of the Big Five film studios of Hollywood's Golden Age, and they eventually went bankrupt and ended in 1957. The problem is many, but the biggest: is the lack of a winning strategy when 'their chips were down." One can go from the top of the world to nothing without clear sight of the road ahead and some degree of humility when things are going well. This method can be used not just for business, but also for personal growth and, well, personal development. If you do the same workout of your arms every day the body begins to learn and is unchallenged and the growth stops. So one has to be flexible, and re-strategize things in life to avoid declines in personal career growth, personal health, or even relationships.

7. Ask Strategic Questions

A lot of great ideas come from, "What happens if..." To blossom as a critical thinker, pertinent questions should be asked. Not just for business, but how you can improve yourself and your career strategy. According to the Harvard Business School course 'Disruptive Strategy" simply asking questions can bring forth opportunities if you are stuck in a predicament. It can remove the veil of ambiguity and shed the light on being enlightened to a new idea. You can ask questions about how you can position yourself in the market, new growth, where you will be in five years, or how the competition will grow in your field. There are many questions you could ask yourself related to the company you want to start or even yourself to improve. Form a dialogue with your inner mind to ask questions of 'what if' and then put forth a strategy, short-term, medium-term, long term that will lead to ultimate success.

8. Study Contrasting Ideas

Sometimes people with opposite opinions on yourself may have some good ideas there because of their life experience. With growth you can learn to change and adapt your way of thinking, and doors can open with new ventures to explore. Thinking of that devil's advocate personality that maybe they have some ideas in there, maybe not all of them, but some of them can be used. Do not be opposed to a good idea just because you didn't think of it first. A good example is CEO Steve Job, and Apple is known for building its own computers, the hardware, and the software, from the ground up so it seamlessly works with one another. From that, the software and hardware are harmonious and bring forth a better user experience as it cuts out the middleman software. Bill Gates's Microsoft is diametrically opposite. It took an approach of just licensing their software out, and third-party companies like Dell and Sony build the actual computer and they, in fact, would load the computer with their own software too, in addition to Microsoft's Windows. What that did, is cut down on the profit Microsoft earned as they were for the longest time purely a software company and also made the user experience less like a Frankenstein computer of different company's ideas. In the later 2010s, Microsoft studied Apple and how their strategy is not exactly market share, but rather… profit and of course high end-user experience. They saw the iPad as a shattering threat to their business empire and they changed course. So Microsoft now makes their own Microsoft computers now… something they have never done in their entire company history. Over decades, and seeing the massive rise of Apple, they changed their tune, looked at contrasting ideas, and learned that Steve Jobs's love for software and hardware synchronization brings forth just a better computer. That also, in the same token of breath, brings forth more profit to the company too. The moral of this story is, sometimes people who have different ideas than you… could have a better idea if you studied their insight.

9. School and Training Or Youtube Training

This is kind of a no-brainer. There are certain careers where formal training is key. Big lucrative jobs in any health field require extra training. But even for artistic careers, we don't necessarily need to spend a whole fortune of money, you could take some type of courses to learn different skills that you are not fully developed in. Another avenue to explore is what is en vogue right now among young and old: Youtube tutorials. There is Harvard education right on Youtube for free where one can learn just about anything from Neuroplasticity, and astrophysics, to how the pyramids were built by putting on stones on sleds or just about any topic to become an informed person in the field. But Youtube does not give you that stamp of approval a degree does on the resume, whereas a formal degree may be a great asset to your development as a person (and also boost self-esteem, which is a key to anything in life.) In terms of developing skills in creative fields, learning about history, research, writing, and self-care, YouTube is an impeccable resort to develop your psyche and understanding of the world.

10. Search for Ideas

Keep your eyes peeled and your ears and mind open for what your next idea can be. Sometimes imitation is a great source of finding new ideas and directions to take. But many ideas can spring out of nowhere on casual walks, reading 'out of-comfort zone books, in the bath, or maybe even watching a movie. Ideas are everywhere and can Germinate... in your subconscious and also consciousness. Where maybe you 'saw' or heard something but never really thought about it. Weeks, months, or even years down the line, you may spark a new idea by just encountering something different. Fresh ideas sometimes come from not following the beaten path but also can come from 'meditative' type states when you're just casually doing stuff.

11. WRITING DOWN YOUR GOALS

Marshall Arts icon Bruce Lee wrote himself a letter that he could become a Hollywood star. It was an affirmation to himself, he could become one. According to the Dominican University of California, People with actionable goals written down are 42% more likely to achieve them. Write down short-term goals, and write down long-term goals, but put them on paper (or digital file) and update them often with new things that are working and not working. Give yourself positive reinforcement that XY worked, and maybe XX didn't work. Writing is a good way to cement an action plan that you could formulate in reality. Have one-year dreams, next year's dreams, next year's dreams (et cetera.) Map our journey, like a hero's journey, like Frodo in Lord of the Rings heading to Mount Doom to destroy the One Ring. If you are filled with ambiguity about how to finish your goal, then you are troubled to actually do it. Follow that morning star of your goal-writing, every day, that you formulated as something tangibly realistic that you can achieve.

Marshall Arts icon Bruce Lee wrote himself a letter that he could become a Hollywood star. It was an affirmation to himself, he could become one. According to the Dominican University of California, People with actionable goals written down are 42% more likely to achieve them. Write down short-term goals, and write down long-term goals, but put them on paper (or digital file) and update them often with new things that are working and not working. Give yourself positive reinforcement that XY worked, and maybe XX didn't work. Writing is a good way to cement an action plan that you could formulate in reality. Have one-year dreams, next year's dreams, next year's dreams (et cetera.) Map our journey, like a hero's journey, like Frodo in Lord of the Rings heading to Mount Doom to destroy the One Ring. If you are filled with ambiguity about how to finish your goal, then you are troubled to actually do it. Follow that morning star of your goal-writing, every day, that you formulated as something tangibly realistic that you can achieve

12. Write Any Other Ideas Somewhere

In the modern age thanks to so much technology, there are numerous ways to forget a great idea. The answer: notes. Sometimes less great ideas you write down can suddenly become great ideas when you are in a different, more confident mood. Though this author is a writer and naturally writes ideas, using that technique for even working as a manager, where your eyes are open for flaws, you can write down a fix so you never forget. Depending on your field of study, this may do nothing for that career. But for other improvements in life, fixing character flaws, and writing down ideas is a good strategy.

13. Envision Your Idealized Self

If you are feeling dissolution, try this: visualize. In the occipital lobe is the visual cortex and which is a key part of the brain to use.

How? Well, If you want to become a big alpha dog CEO, rich, liked, with tons of communicating skills—-it starts with imagination, you can. Forming an inner belief in yourself that you do something by seeing yourself as that, will help crystalize it into reality. If you are filled with woe is me, I'm not good enough, and never will be good enough i.e., fixed mindset, then you are in a world of trouble. Another thing to consider, which there are many mentions of, is a thing called a vision board. Which is a collage of images cut out of a magazine or articles, printed out, and pasted on cardboard to represent your idealization self. The way you can see that board and visualize it. If you want to be a published writer, for instance, visualize yourself as one that you could be if you put in the effort, research, and action plan. Essentially that is: mental rehearsal for actually achieving it. Just remember to take into account the above-named parts about dream killing failure and reacting to it accordingly for this mental rehearsal.

14. Develop an Exponential Mindset

Short term, people overestimate what they can do. Long term, they underestimate what they can do. Growth takes gradual and steady improvements and overnight success, focusing on what's important for growth and ignoring the rest. To believe in change, block out distinctions, and look at your growth as a person/company over a longer arc than short-period gains. It is to think of oneself a bit like a stock, where yes there are times when things plummet, but over the course of many years, the growth is there. Example: the total Dow Jones stock market value on January 1st, 1962 was 724.71. Flash forward 50 years to January 1st, 2022, and it's at 36,585.06. In a nutshell, it comes down to incremental thinking of small steady moves, factoring in failure, and the instant of some overnight Powerball Lottery winning success. The former is more likely and achievable.

15. Early Bird Is First to the Worm

American polymath and founding father, Benjamin Franklin was a quintessential early riser and planned his day by getting up at 5 a.m. That gave him ample time to be a polymath personality to pursue things like science, writing, inventing, and philosophizing. If everybody in your freelancer field is starting their day at 8 am, but you are at 11 AM, that gives your competition an advantage. Start your day early or, in a normal time frame. Ultra-successful people get a leg up on the combination by just starting their day sooner. Other benefits are less traffic, and you can have simple 'me time to take in information from the previous day to formulate a plan that day. There are strong benefits to early rising but, as you may remember from the previous chapter, not at the expense of getting proper sleep. So if you wanna be an early riser make sure you go to bed at a proper time and make sure you have a full restorative sleep during that time.

16. Innovate When You Can

It takes a long of brazen audacity to do something that is how of the box thinking. All great inventions come from that mental framework of doing something different. Serbian-American futuristic and pioneering inventor, Nikola Tesla invented the alternating current from the time-tested 'direct current.' All breakouts are about thinking a bit differently from the herd. Another example is Amazon, where in the mid-90s, there were no online booksellers to pick up your copy of Jurassic Park. So Jeff Bezos created that and, bit by bit, using many of the above techniques, saw steady improvement in the innovative idea of an online marketplace. The reality is many people are in a fixed mindset, and if you adopt a growth mindset and then look to innovate, you can devise a unique strategy for innovation. Just don't put all your chickens in one basket, have a fallback plan on said innovation, and think of ways to overcome if something doesn't take off immediately. Another more recent example would be From that historical blunder of this, Japanese video game titan Nintendo. In 2012 they rereleased their least successful home console ever: the polarizing and misunderstood Wii U. Which was a video game system with an unwieldy tablet-like screen that looked unsightly. They wanted mobile and home but at the same time. Nintendo was in dire straits, and its stock and market share were decimated from its previous ultra-successful Wii system. What they did: they learned from failure and made a system, the Switch, that is a home console to play on the tv and then gets taken out of the dock to be played on the go. Nintendo learned from its failures with the Wii U, reworked it, make it more accessible, devised a straightforward name, and created most likely their most successful console of all time in terms of sales. Failure and re-strategizing can bring about innovation and unheard success.

8.2 Summary

One does not need to be the world chess champion Magnus Carlsen being good at strategy. Many people in life don't formulate any kind of strategy and are moving through life like a leaf in the wind. Devising a strategy for your life, career, and love life, and making sure it is realistic, thoughtful, and able to adapt to changes, is key to achieving what you want. Just don't use these time-tested strategies to conquer Europe like Napoleon Bonaparte or anything.

Chapter 9: Wandering Mind - DMN/TPN Mode, and How To Switch

Famed Psychiatrist Sigmund Freud taught about how the dynamic subconscious can affect our day-to-day lives. He studies various therapeutic techniques of how things we aren't thinking about control our day-to-day lives. He revolutionized psychiatry by studying the subconscious and Psychoanalysis. We hear that studying is the part where we are shut off to introspection, and our brain is kind of on autopilot. Everybody daydreams. When you are sitting at work thinking about that trip to Venice Beach California. Or that time you fell in love with somebody you shouldn't have. Or simple pleasures like a French Silk Pie. Or maybe you have Chronomentrophobia, a fear of clocks and or the more common fear of time itself. Whatever is glowing in your brain during the day. But sometimes non-commandeered thoughts can affect you from being productive in life and....happiness. One must have the presence in mind when to turn the switch to OFF. First, from various research in 2001 by scientist Marcus Raichle, M.D, let's learn the distinctions between DMN and PTN.

What Is DMN (Default Mode Network)?

This is layman's terms: a time with the brain is resting and controlling high-order functions. A more medical explanation: This is a part of the brain that is a loose connection with neurons and spontaneously reacts to various areas of the brain in 'passive moments.'. Let's first explain a bit about the interworking of the brain and how much it encompasses. The part of the brain that has DMN temporal lobe, prefrontal cortex, the posterior cingulate cortex. All of these are parts of the brain that are in charge of memory (prefrontal), ranging emotions and thoughts towards goals (posterior cingulate), autobiographical memorization, and the ability to reflect from the posterior cingulate. In a microcosm: this part of the brain that controls various emotional states, introspection, mind-wondering, long-term memory, Attention Deficit Disorder (A.D.D.), and hyperactivity. By Sigmund Freud's definition, this would be the subconscious mind and also the preconscious mind and daydreaming.

Positive Constructive Day-Dreaming

These constant wishful thoughts like the aforementioned trip to Vegas California, or having a French Silk pie, or dreaming about being an elementary school teacher. All positive and somewhat productive thoughts swirl in one's brain. These—-in moderation—-are good to have to go in your head.

Guilty-Dysphoric Daydreaming

When your brain is full of tempestuous rumination thoughts in your head. Negative Nancy. Woe is me. The pessimist. Or maybe something serious is going on, like Post Traumatic Stress Disorder from serving. The counterproductive thoughts that bog down your day, like being stuck in wet cement.

Poor Attention Control Daydreaming

 This is when you have a hard time concentrating on work, and your mind is filled with a random, sometimes fragmented web of thoughts. This affects your work, communication skills, and happiness. It is equally bad as the above one and may require meditation and/or medication.

What Is a Task-positive Network (TPN)?

This is part of the brain related to focus and would be tied closely to Sigmund Freud's conscious mind. We are actively doing something and keenly aware of it, like, well, writing a book on TPN, for instance. You are actively playing basketball. Or within a conversation with a co-worker. It's where you need razor-like concentration and then uses short-term memory to make snap decisions. Within your mode of consciousness, you are happier than if you are just 'there' like the above. Distinguishing these two methods of thought is important to know how to regulate your emotions and your behavior.

The Underlying Problem:

The two modes of thought are at odds with one another, like Dr. Jekyll or Mr. Hyde. When one is active, the other is less active. If you don't have a present to mind to know when you are DMN parts of the brain can creep in like a wandering toddler. It also hinders you from living a balanced and productive life where your subconscious is starting to rule you. According to research from American psychologist Richard J. Davidson, the average American spends 47% of the time not paying attention to what they are doing. A wandering daydreaming mind could use a lasso to reign in so you can be more productive and more balanced. Studies have found there to be a link between DMN mode and depression and that meditation to get the brain to get out of that thinking pattern, can snap one out of Default Mode Activity of depressing daydreams of lack of concentration. The person's default mode of their brain is about various factors, nature (DNA) vs. nurture (how they learned to cope), and every person, just like the unique contours of their face, is different. So the best answer is to be aware of your DMN, how you respond to your feelings, and learn methods to the brain from depressing or counter-productive thought patterns that spiral down like a kamikaze pilot. People who sticker with chronic depression would especially be beneficial from meditation to augment their thinking patterns for their welfare. The problem with daydreamers and writers having a natural skill is that it is tied to both depression and creativity. Over the course of time, researchers have found three types of daydreamers. And the types of daydreams from when the brain is in DMN are a lot like Dr. Jekyll and Mr. Hyde of the brain.

Correlation Between DMN and Empathy

Understanding emotions is critical in understanding social situations. Understanding social cues, body language, minor changes in voice, reading faces, and just the indirectness of some social interventions is important. There have been various clinical studies using fMRI machines to determine a greater understanding of our minds. Our cognitive empathy part of our brain connects and overlaps with the Default Mode Network of the brain. This means if you are an overzealous DMN, be it from depression, injury, or neurological disorder, in your brain, your perception of others may be thrown askew. The simple understanding: your brain is more focused on itself, like narcissism, than it is on others' feelings. As various meditation gurus would say: you're simply not 'not present.' Now there is a Scientific Neuroimaging understanding of what exactly they're not present in. To have your empathy firing on all cylinders and you are fully reading people and connecting to people, one has to understand when to put their grips on that DMN in the brain or you will have a social disconnection from your peers. If you want to connect better and be that social butterfly, put a lasso on that DMN.

Default Mode Network and Neurological Disorders

If you are not controlling this part of your brain, you can exacerbate negative feelings. First, you are susceptible to developing severe depression and then hyperactivity and have bipolar disorder and PTSD (Post Traumatic Stress Disorder).

Learn to control your DMN to thwart or reduce the chances of many neurological disorders. Having an out-of-balance DMN is tied to many white matter abnormalities and neuropsychiatric disorders. Various studies and neuroimaging found information on the following neurodevelopmental disorders:

Attention Deficit Hyperactivity Disorder (ADHD)

Research has shown that people with ADHD have less DMN connection in the brain. There is a decreased activity where the brain is a DMN. It also causes negative effects on the ability of self-reflection for a long period of time.

Autism (ASD)

The same can be said with people with autism and understanding social cues, there is a correlation between the two and their effects on DMN within the resting state.

PTSD (Post Traumatic Stress Disorder)

Finally, clinical studies of PTSD also have abnormalities in the brain in the DMN. There has been a severe change in what is going on in the Brain chemistry during DMN. The effects of DMN on people who are mentally scared with PTSD are striking.

Chronic Pain

People with chronic pain show they have high DMN activity in the brain. The pain modulatory system systems are, understandably, highly active, and that ties into the DMN network, where they are mentally 'checking out.'

Schizophrenia

Clinically research showed that people with Schizophrenia are more active with DMN. Meaning their 'restful' state of the brain is more out of balance and thus controlling the person. When there are tasks that require attention, the DMN is unusually active. When that is reduced, TPN (when the brain focuses) does reduce the DMN. Also, other neurological disorders in people with schizophrenia is paranoia, and they also have high DMN while they are actively trying to have razor-like focus using TPN.

Alzheimer's Disease

Most people know what this is, the reduction of the brain acting by way of toxic beta-amyloid 42 plagues build up. What these plagues do is collect between neurons in your brain. The result: they disrupt cell function and affect memory and motor skills. But what has been discovered through clinical research, is the reduction of brain acuity goes into the Default Mode Network too. Antecedent factors, meaning—-what is triggering, appear to be negative balanced DMN that appears to be the first steps to having this neurodegeneration in the brain. If you want to keep your brain avoiding this, be mindful of abnormalities in your DMN.

9.1 Tips on How To Switch How Out of DMN

The first step is recognizing you may have a problem with 'not being present and DMN. What you can do is try rote learning, which is a repetitive behavior that forges is deeply embedded learning. It is a memorization technique for doing the same thing again and again. There are many things one can do to lessen the consequences of having an overactive DMN mode. Each time you are within DMN and your mind is in la-la land, and you understand it, implement steps and habitual patterns to switch out of it each time. Do not stay locked in your head but rather in action to control your mind rambunctious mind with these steps

Stay Motivated

If you have a profession doing highly repetitive work, try to find something you can do for many hours that stimulates your mind. Doing the same thing every day, be it cleaning floors, or changing light bulbs, doesn't use much cognitive function and puts you into a DMN and just zone out it's the Alpha Centauri galaxy. Seek mentally stimulating things around people or changing work that you can interact with, not just be sucked into the Twilight Zone of television.

Meditation

Rigorous methods have found that practicing mindfulness and meditation can lessen the effects of DMN overpowering your day-to-day life. It's worth noting that T.M. or Transcendental Medication, in particular, can reduce the negative neurological consequences of DMN. From Zen to Mindfulness to Qigong, anything meditation will help.

Acupuncture

Brain Imaging with fMRI (Functional magnetic resonance imaging) has found that the ancient method of needles into the skin can help alleviate distracting DMN thoughts. It distracts you with minor pain across the body, so you are focused on the here and now for long periods. Throughout many sessions, you could have positive results.

Medication

Taking some type of meditation for focusing, like Citalopram, Escitalopram, and Fluoxetine can help with regaining focus and reducing that out-of-alignment DMN. Ketamine, in particular, disturbs the frontal lobe DMN, which will help other parts of the brain control get out of the stranglehold of subconscious control.

Psychedelics

Over the years, magic mushrooms have proven to have many health benefits besides listening to Pink Floyd's Dark Side of The Moon. The National Library of Medicine did a study on Hallucinogenic mushrooms called psilocybin and LSD on the brain. These types of psychedelics have been used for centuries in healing. They found that it reduces the lesser the connections of DMN by way of temporally "ego-dissolution" by losing the senses when using these substances and creating changes in personality. Essentially, what happens when taking Magic Mushroom: the brain becomes more interconnected. They also found this method is good for people with depression and other neurological disorders.

9.2 Summary

One does not need to be exactly Sigmund Freud to understand how the subconscious will affect your consciousness——for good or ill. These are various techniques to Shepard focus in your life and also have a presence of mind of your DMN. Having at least a basic understanding of how DMN and TPN form the various interacting brain regions for good or bad. Make changes to your self-awareness within yourself to be on the first step for a powerful transformation of who you can be. How you handle your DMN can leave a lasting impact of who you are... or will become. The key to unlocking being locked in your mind is being aware of it.

Chapter 10: ADHD - Deep Look Into the ADHD Brain in Children and Adults

If you are a person with a wandering mind, restless, can't concentrate for long periods, and a bit unruly when forced to be confined, that is a tall tale sign of ADHD. Or, in non-acronym terms: attention deficit hyperactivity disorder. If you are a person who has this—well—- you are not alone.

The facts: there are 3 million cases in the United States cases per year with ADHD. The list of truly exceptional people is quite staggering. Including record-winning gold medal list Olympian Michael Phelps. So does comedian Howie Mandel from America's Got Talent. So does 2016 gymnastic gold medallist Simone Biles. Hip-hop/producer Black Eyed Peas member will.i.am. Renowned political analyst James Carville. In just about every field you can imagine, people can have ADHD, and also the same token, breathing excels in life.

Many people grow out of adulthood, but some people still have it as they get older. 8.4 percent of kids and 2.5% of adults have attention deficit disorder. Within the United States, it is estimated that 6.4 kids between the ages of four and seventeen have been diagnosed with affliction. Within the western parts of the United States are the lowest cases, the Scientific reason for that is unclear but could be a contributor to the weather. Within the coldest region of the country, the Midwest is more prevalent where many states are unusually high compared to others. This could mean, from this writer's perspective, there could be some correlation between the two. Kentucky has the highest rate at 14.8% of kids. While the lowest rate, just so happens to be the hottest state with Nevada at 4.2%. Other states are California at 5.9% and Arkansas, Louisiana, and Indiana, all around 14.6% and 13.3%. But generally, midwestern states are hit the heaviest with this problem with kids. If you are from these necks of the woods, and you have a hard time focusing and are restless, you may have ADHD. Nevertheless, this disorder is an epidemic of proportions in certain regions of the country and affects people's entire lives.

10.1 So What Is ADHD?

Well, it's the difficulty concentrating, essentially, and acting impulsive. Adults with this affliction may have low self-esteem and hypersensitivity to criticism. If you are a person who can't still, fidgets, and your mind is in dreamland a lot in the aforementioned DMN, that is a good example of what ADHD is. The problems are not from being defiant and not generally about the person understanding the directions given either. And if you are a person with ADHD, here's some rocket fuel motivation that you can still accomplish anything you put your mind to: according to Michael Phelps, the winner of the most gold medals in Olympic history, his teachers told him, "I had a teacher tell me that I would never amount to anything and I would never be successful."

Those sometimes tough love could motivate a kid, that teacher's brutal assessment of him was completely off the mark and uncalled for. So what gets into the medical understanding of what precisely is ADHD.

The three types of neurobehavioral disorders for ADHD are:

Predominantly inattentive presentation - This is when you have difficulty concentrating or can't sustain attention, procrastinate, and just have general forgetfulness. Has difficulty completing work and mind wonders, and they misplace things.

Predominantly hyperactive/impulsive presentation - This is about the movement of your body and just being hyperactive. Restlessness, fidgeting, talking too much, and just being impulsive decisions.

Combined presentation.
This is when you have all of the symptoms combined.

Other things to consider not ADHD:

(ODD) Oppositional Defiant Disorder - This is behavior rider when a child is unruly, and defiant, and harbors hostility towards peers, teachers, and in particular, people within the authority. It is a personality trait of being rebellious.

Autism Disorder

You owe your child to being on the spectrum of an autism disorder which prevents you from socially interacting, learning, and an assortment of other things.

Diagnosis

To adequately determine if you or your child have ADHD, the symptoms need to persist for six months or more. The way it is determined if you or your child have it would be an assessment with a questionnaire by a child or adult psychiatrist. This would involve a series of interview questions and personal reports from other people that encountered the patient. Another thing that would happen to diagnose ADHD, to determine there isn't anything else medically abnormal, is a physical examination by a doctor. The reason why it is cortical to have a physical examination to rule out if there is substance abuse is proven, anxiety, head injury, substance abuse or thyroid issue, neurological mood disorder, or the above (ODD) Oppositional

Defiant Disorder. Or an fMRI could be done on the brain to understand the abnormality in the behavior.

Causes for ADHD

There has been scientific evidence that your very genetics comes into play for underlying causes of ADHD, not just environmental factors such as a chaotic household. But geneticists have not determined what the gene combination is that is the catalyst for the neurological disorder. Using a magnetic field and radio frequencies of MRI of the brain, they have found anatomical differences in reduced gray area and white matter between the brains of children with ADHD and those without. They have also found through brain imaging that the front lobes, caudate nucleus, and cerebellar vermis are different from people with ADHD. Other things that come into play are the child's birth weight, and being born prematurely. Other underlying factors of having toxins in utero such as smoking, lead, or alcohol and the mother having an exorbitant amount of stress while pregnant.
10.2 Ways to Improve From ADHD

1. Medication

There are various treatments for ADHD, from therapy to psychiatric intervention. The first approach is the medication one could take, such as Ridellan. Talking to your physician is best to determine if medication is the best treatment for ADHD or if something like behavior therapy or both is more beneficial. These can help relieve symptoms of ADHD to help the stranglehold it has day to day life. The five types of psychostimulant medication for ADHD are:

Ritalin - AKA methylphenidate
Vyvanse - AKA lisdexamfetamine
Monograph - AKA dexamfetamine

Strattera- AKA atomoxetine

Intuniv- AKA guanfacine

All of these medications have side effects like drowsiness, headaches, vomiting, and diarrhea. Ones like Ritalin have a rapid heartbeat, panic, and could cause heart failure. Consult your doctor on all of these to determine if this is the best route to treat you or your child's ADHD.

Behavior Therapy

According to research from the National Institute of Mental Health, they have found that medication and addition to behavior therapy are the best way to treat ADHD. This study was also reinforced by the American Academy of Pediatrics on the power of the two combination methods. Consult a board-certified physician and a psychiatrist on this method to perhaps make life-changing changes in yourself or your children. These are some Cognitive Behavioral Therapy (CBT) tips from the According to the director Center for Children and Families at UONY William Pelham, Jr., Ph.D., Marsha Linehan, Ph.D., ABPP, a professor of psychology at the University of Washington, Carol Brady, Ph.D., a child psychologist practicing in Houston. The reason is enough for this: a clinical study by Boston's Massachusetts General Hospital, conducted in 2010, found the combination of the two methods brings about the best results.

Therapy #1 - Children: Positive/Negative Reinforcement

Formulate a strategy to control your child's behavior through positive and negative reinforcement. First, devise a reward system for your kid for exemplary behavior. On the flip side, they are dismayed by negative behavior by ignoring it so they don't get attention. The kid might just be acting out to get attention. Snatch away things, such as video games or smartphones, if negative behavior spirals downward. If you find something that causes the unruly behavior, restrict it from the child.

Therapy #2 - Adults: Control DMN/Daydreaming Thoughts

Controlling negative pattern thinking from the subconscious. The DMN, the part of your brain on autopilot, is something that can be controlled to help with ADHD. If your mind is stuck in a loop-a-loop of negative thoughts, then control them by being mindful of them. For some of the more severe issues like hyperactivity, negative pattern thinking, and being impulsive, these techniques won't be 100% a remedy but lessens their impact on them. According to research, there is no evidence that CBT can replace psychostimulant drug therapy, but evidence of these techniques with a combination of a daily capsule can bring about lowering the symptoms.

CHANGE DEFAULT MINDSET TO LESSEN THE IMPACT OF ADHD

Overgeneralization - If you make one mistake, you see it as a pattern and overreact emotionally. One is too hard on oneself for minor human error.

Comparative Thinking - Comparing yourself against unrealistic expectations of others, then feeling inferior. If you are not as good as the greatest, then you are not good at all methods of thinking.

Mind Reading - Believe in you have the ability to clairvoyance. You see people and think the worst they are thinking in reality, their thoughts are more mundane.

Fortune telling - prophecies that things are always turned on badly. The result: it can become a self-fulfilling prophecy because of that.

All-Or-Nothing thinking - This is when you see the totality of everything in extremes of black and white. There is no middle ground. All things are good and bad.

Magnification And Minimization - Believing seller accomplishments in life as minor but believing the minor failures as colossal mistakes.

"Should" statements - Being stubborn, not flexible to have things your own way, which opens the doors for self-criticism and feelings of bitterness.

Therapy #3 - Adults Dialectical Behavior Therapy

Neuro-psychology can be mitigated using Dialectical Behavioral Therapy (DBT). This involves going to weekly support group sessions to develop better-coping skills in social situations. This talk therapy can help improve personality disorders or how you handle interpersonal conflicts. It can be used to lessen mood disorders and self-harm, and suicidal thoughts. DBT can be taught to offer support to those who are struggling in society with personality issues that hold them back and may bring the arm to themselves. It uses various methods like mindfulness and acceptance of oneself and improving self-esteem.

Therapy #4 - Coaching

There are so many aspects in life to learn and a professionally trained coach can help one learn how to handle things better. What are coaches for time management, planning, motivation, being balanced, and making healthy decisions—-is endless. Having a Guiding Light coach person in your life who can support you through thick and thin and a huge way to build self-esteem and learn to modify behavior. There are ones for adults and children who can guide them along through dark passes in life or just give them simple pointers on how to handle situations that may arise.

Therapy #5 - Neurofeedback

This is not the pin eyeballs open and forced to watch the movie "The Ludovico Technique" featured in the Stanley Kubrick movie The Clockwork Orange. Rather than putting something on your head. This is Neurotherapy that uses devices strapped to give biofeedback through an electrode on the head. This is used for impulse control to get them to change their method- of thinking. This can help people from being unruly and help tame their aggressive and counterproductive personality traits. The jury is still out on clinical research if this works or not.

Therapy #6 - Play Therapy

This method is simply being playful with your children to get them to relax, bond with them, reduce anxiety and improve self-esteem. Many children, perhaps the middle child, can somewhat feel left out if there is somebody born after them or before them. (Research the middle child syndrome.) For your child to feel hopeful, happy, and with self-esteem, they must play and also bond with their parents through playtime. So if you get left alone a lot and have problems in school, maybe it's time to bond with them more and play some Nintendo or pick-up basketball with them.

Therapy #7 - Music Therapy

Music does a lot more than just getting your head to bob up and down through a stimulating melody—the psychological effects also help focus, be hyper, and develop social skills and memory. This helps with cognitive ability and helps produce neurons for neuroplasticity. It also brings pleasure which helps the pleasure hormone, dopamine, rise in the brain. Other things music can do is reduce anxiety, and blood pressure would assist a person to relax, learn and be a more socially skilled member of society. "Listen For Life" founder Donna Stoering gave a Ted Conference about how beneficial music is to regulating emotions, helping to sleep, and especially beneficially for somebody with hyperactivity disorder: calming rage. Finally, a clinic done in 2020 found Music therapy improves attentiveness in children.

Therapy #8 - Art Therapy

There is this thing called Right Brain Left Brain and Its Relevance to Art. Which means the left brain is more into math and language. The right brain is more art. Some children, and adults, are simply more right-brain dominant thinkers and that is what they are interested in. Meanwhile, many things in life are not art in the slightest, and their minds wander. The solution: Doing anything artistic to help focus concentration. If you have a passion for your project, then your focus only increases exponentially. That is why creating art can help a child or an adult hone their focusing skills. In your wandering mind, children are taught to give razor-like focus on things they enjoy, which can help them develop acuity for other things. Other things art does help deal with emotionally and develop a problem-solving need for everyday life.

Therapy #9 - Equine Therapy

This is one of the more esoteric ones, but there is scientific data on this treatment. Predator animals like dogs and cats hide their feelings to hint. Other prey animals, like horses and donkeys, express their feelings. National Library of Medicine, gave some input on this published study that horseback riding with 5 children helped them improve ADHD. They found that therapeutic horseback had a positive effect on their mental health; instead of simply talking to somebody about their problem, they bonded with animals. There are various activities you can do with a horse, such as Hippotherapy by using the very moment of the horse to improve mental health. Other ones are Therapeutic driving where you would just write the horse with a carriage attached to it. Though, for the everyday child, or the everyday adult, finding the horse to ride may not be realistic. But if you live on a farm somewhere and have some steeds, consider taking a gallop.

Therapy #10 - Video Game Therapy

If the last one about horsing sounds a little bit esoteric and a pipe dream treatment, this one is more realistic for most kids, and would love to hear it. In a Study at Duke by Scott Kollins, a professor in psychiatry and behavioral sciences, he found video games are not an alternative treatment for ADHD but are 'promising.' The study found that kids that took no medication and then played video games 25 minutes a week showed a huge improvement in attention scores, according to Dr. Kollins. It makes sense: video games, especially the more competitive online ones like Call of Duty, take an extraordinary amount of concentration for perhaps dozens of hours to even get adequate at.

10.3 Summary

From controlling DMN to self-help groups to medication to video games, to even riding horses, there are various forms of treatment for ADHD. These techniques and medications could help improve someone who has attention deficit disorder and live a better, more successful life. So whether you are young, old, or in between, if you're a person that struggles with concentration, now is the time to take control of that and live up to your maximum potential so you can reach the Mount Everest of happiness.

Closing Thoughts

This book was compiled through various clinical studies and articles written on the Internet to improve one's mind and outlook on life. Just like a lot of things in life, not everything is a one size fits all method. So there are certain things in this book that will work well for you and your personality, but other things may not quite be cohesive with who you are as a person.

From my personal experience as someone who works as a writer, some of the best things you could do to improve yourself are to have a lifelong love for reading, exercise, diet, and keeping a positive mentality through the trials and tribulations of life. If there is one thing in this book that you could take out there that will most transform, like a moth to a butterfly, and get you out of that turtle shell: the extraordinary and straightforward information from Dr. Carol Dweck's growth mindset versus a fixed mindset study. It is this sobering realization, that you are not fixed at birth from your intelligence and abilities, and if you are weak in an area so be it. Anything else, you can grow exponentially by creating a positive pattern and doing it every single day. Through stride and strife, overcoming hurdles with determination, you could become a better, more emotionally balanced person with incremental improvement. The mindset of personal growth is transformative, and understanding it is not exactly high-brow neuroscience either. That's the difference between progression in life, and being shackled by the iron grip of worrying about failure and slowly regressing backward to depression. As someone who has grown considerably since he got out of college, that was truly the distinguishing factor from my personal growth and a lot of my peers in my youth. Many of the people I grew up with, some white graduated high school, or even college, and kind of gave up on gradually improving on various things in their life. Understanding what person you and those around you and what kind of frame of mind they are in, will help you spearhead forward in life.

In closing, I truly wish you the best in your pursuit to expand your mind and perhaps greater, sunnier horizons through various techniques found in this book. I sincerely thank you for reading and hope these words inspired you to follow your dreams with steadfast passion through pitfalls. In the wise words of Walt Disney, "All of our dreams can come true, if we have the courage to pursue them."

RESOURCES:

INTRODUCTION

Brain plasticity. Brain Plasticity - an overview | ScienceDirect Topics. (n.d.). Retrieved October 28, 2022, from https://www.sciencedirect.com/topics/neuroscience/brain-plasticity

Encyclopædia Britannica, inc. (n.d.). Neuroplasticity. Encyclopædia Britannica. Retrieved October 28, 2022, from https://www.britannica.com/science/neuroplasticity

University, H. (2013, December 16). The 'Mozart effect' of having kids study music? it's only a myth, researchers find. The Washington Post. Retrieved October 28, 2022, from https://www.washingtonpost.com/national/health-science/the-mozart-effect-of-having-kids-study-music-its-only-a-myth-researchers-find/2013/12/13/bd2ede46-6351-11e3-a373-0f9f2d1c2b61_story.html

CHAPTER ONE

Cherry, K. (n.d.). Neuroplasticity: How experience changes the brain. Verywell Mind. Retrieved October 28, 2022, from https://www.verywellmind.com/what-is-brain-plasticity-2794886

Caverzasio, S., Amato, N., Manconi, M., Prosperetti, C., Kaelin-Lang, A., Hutchison, W. D., & Galati, S. (2017, December 24). Brain plasticity and sleep: Implication for movement disorders. Neuroscience & Biobehavioral Reviews. Retrieved October 28, 2022, from https://www.sciencedirect.com/science/article/abs/pii/S0149763417305109

Cherry, K. (n.d.). Neuroplasticity: How experience changes the brain. Verywell Mind. Retrieved October 28, 2022, from https://www.verywellmind.com/what-is-brain-plasticity-2794886

Levine, H. (2022, July 29). 5 brain exercises that Can keep your mind sharp. AARP. Retrieved October 28, 2022, from https://www.aarp.org/health/brain-health/info-2022/workouts-for-brain-health.html

Wikimedia Foundation. (2022, October 13). Neuroplasticity. Wikipedia. Retrieved October 28, 2022, from https://en.wikipedia.org/wiki/Neuroplasticity

Person. (2020, June 17). How to rewire your brain: 6 neuroplasticity exercises. Healthline. Retrieved October 28, 2022, from https://www.healthline.com/health/rewiring-your-brain#travel

Kaplan, E. (2017, December 26). How to rewire your brain for massive success, according to Neuroscience. Medium. Retrieved October 28, 2022, from https://medium.com/thrive-global/how-to-rewire-your-brain-for-massive-success-according-to-neuroscience-f051a30395d1

Mark Stibich, P. D. (2020, March 2). Top 10 ways to improve your brain fitness. Verywell Mind. Retrieved October 28, 2022, from https://www.verywellmind.com/top-ways-to-improve-your-brain-fitness-2224137

Is literacy declining?: Inside higher ed. Higher Ed Gamma. (n.d.). Retrieved October 28, 2022, from https://www.insidehighered.com/blogs/higher-ed-gamma/literacy-declining

S;, C. R. M. A. C. (n.d.). N-3 fatty acids: Role in neurogenesis and neuroplasticity. Current medicinal chemistry. Retrieved October 28, 2022, from https://pubmed.ncbi.nlm.nih.gov/23746276/

Zhang L;Luo J;Zhang M;Yao W;Ma X;Yu SY; (n.d.). Effects of curcumin on chronic, unpredictable, mild, stress-induced depressive-like behaviour and structural plasticity in the lateral amygdala of rats. The international journal of neuropsychopharmacology. Retrieved October 28, 2022, from https://pubmed.ncbi.nlm.nih.gov/24405689/

Sisson, M. (2021, August 24). 16 ways to increase neuroplasticity (and why that's important). Mark's Daily Apple. Retrieved October 28, 2022, from https://www.marksdailyapple.com/16-ways-to-increase-neuroplasticity-and-why-thats-important/

Moore, Z., Kemberling, C., Barlow, S., Saito, E., & Jeffrey Edwards, P. D. (n.d.). Effects of the ketogenic diet on learning and memory. BYU ScholarsArchive. Retrieved October 28, 2022, from https://scholarsarchive.byu.edu/library_studentposters_2021/25/

Rossi, E., Cheng, H., Kroll, J. F., Diaz, M. T., & Newman, S. D. (2017, November 21). Changes in white-matter connectivity in late Second Language Learners: Evidence from diffusion tensor imaging. Frontiers in psychology. Retrieved October 28, 2022, from https://www.ncbi.nlm.nih.gov/pmc/articles/PMC5702476/

CHAPTER TWO

Sur, S. (2022, October 27). Winning mentality: 10 secrets to developing & maintaining it. Wealthful Mind. Retrieved October 28, 2022, from https://wealthfulmind.com/winning-mentality-secrets-to-developing-it/#:~:text=A%20winning%20mentality%20is%20a,seeks%20growth%20in%20every%20opportunity.

How to surround yourself with good people in your life. tonyrobbins.com. (n.d.). Retrieved October 28, 2022, from https://www.tonyrobbins.com/stories/business-mastery/surround-yourself-with-quality-people/

U.S. Department of Health and Human Services. (n.d.). Alcohol's damaging effects on the brain. National Institute on Alcohol Abuse and Alcoholism. Retrieved October 28, 2022, from https://pubs.niaaa.nih.gov/publications/aa63/aa63.htm

Pearson, J., Naselaris, T., Holmes, E. A., & Kosslyn, S. M. (2015, October). Mental imagery: Functional mechanisms and clinical applications. Trends in cognitive sciences. Retrieved October 28, 2022, from https://www.ncbi.nlm.nih.gov/pmc/articles/PMC4595480/

NBA. (2022, June 14). Final 4:39 of Michael Jordan's last Bulls Game vs jazz - 1998 NBA Finals. YouTube. Retrieved October 28, 2022, from https://www.youtube.com/watch?v=VlbC8q4VkL4

Wikimedia Foundation. (2022, October 28). Tom Brady. Wikipedia. Retrieved October 28, 2022, from https://en.wikipedia.org/wiki/Tom_Brady

Campbell, S. (2016, October 13). 10 ways to develop an unshakable belief in yourself. Entrepreneur. Retrieved October 28, 2022, from https://www.entrepreneur.com/living/10-ways-to-develop-an-unshakable-belief-in-yourself/283645

CHAPTER THREE

Mayo Foundation for Medical Education and Research. (2022, February 3). How to stop negative self-talk. Mayo Clinic. Retrieved October 28, 2022, from https://www.mayoclinic.org/healthy-lifestyle/stress-management/in-depth/positive-thinking/art-20043950

Mayo Foundation for Medical Education and Research. (2021, July 29). Stress relief from laughter? it's no joke. Mayo Clinic. Retrieved October 28, 2022, from https://www.mayoclinic.org/healthy-lifestyle/stress-management/in-depth/stress-relief/art-20044456

The neuroscience of breaking out of negative thinking (and ... - inc.com. (n.d.). Retrieved October 28, 2022, from https://www.inc.com/nate-klemp/try-this-neuroscience-based-technique-to-shift-your-mindset-from-negative-to-positive-in-30-seconds.html

M.D., C. B. (2021, August 17). 85% of what you worry about never happens. Medium. Retrieved October 28, 2022, from https://medium.com/mind-cafe/85-of-what-you-worry-about-never-happens-3f748aab16de

Cho, J. (2016, December 28). The science behind how Mindfulness can help break negative thought patterns. Forbes. Retrieved October 28, 2022, from https://www.forbes.com/sites/jeenacho/2016/12/27/the-science-behind-how-mindfulness-helps-you-to-break-negative-thought-patterns/?sh=68c751db4119

Team, B. and S. (2022, March 11). How to turn around your negative thinking. Cleveland Clinic. Retrieved October 28, 2022, from https://health.clevelandclinic.org/turn-around-negative-thinking/

Morris, L. (2022, March 11). 3 ways to turn negative into positive. wikiHow. Retrieved October 28, 2022, from https://www.wikihow.com/Turn-Negative-Into-Positive

Clark, D. (n.d.). 3 ways to turn negativity into positivity. TTI Success Insights Blog. Retrieved October 28, 2022, from https://blog.ttisi.com/3-ways-to-turn-negativity-into-positivity

Writer. (n.d.). When nothing's funny, even simulated laughter can be good medicine. Home. Retrieved October 28, 2022, from https://www.globallymealliance.org/blog/when-nothings-funny-even-simulated-laughter-can-be-good-medicine

Substance abuse and mental health services administration. SAMHSA. (n.d.). Retrieved October 28, 2022, from https://www.samhsa.gov/

Bradshaw, F. (2022, April 8). How to turn negative thoughts into positive actions. Mind Tools Blog. Retrieved October 28, 2022, from https://www.mindtools.com/blog/how-to-turn-negative-thoughts-into-positive-actions/

The real health benefits of smiling and laughing. The Real Health Benefits of Smiling and Laughing | SCL Health. (n.d.). Retrieved

October 28, 2022, from https://www.sclhealth.org/blog/2019/06/the-real-health-benefits-of-smiling-and-laughing/

Building Self-esteem: A Self-Help Guide, SAMHSA booklet SMA-3715. (n.d.). Building Self-Esteem by Changing Negative Thoughts. Building self-esteem by changing negative thoughts. Retrieved October 28, 2022, from https://www.mentalhelp.net/self-esteem/changing-negative-thoughts/

Santos-Longhurst, A. (2019, February 21). How to think positive and have an optimistic outlook: 8 tips. Healthline. Retrieved October 28, 2022, from https://www.healthline.com/health/how-to-think-positive#overview

https://academic.oup.com/aje/article/185/1/21/2631298

CHAPTER FOUR

The power of yet: Carol S Dweck: TED Conference. YouTube. (2014, September 12). Retrieved October 28, 2022, from https://youtu.be/J-swZaKN2Ic

FutureLearn. (2022, April 25). What is a growth mindset and how can you develop one? FutureLearn. Retrieved October 28, 2022, from https://www.futurelearn.com/info/blog/general/develop-growth-mindset

Fensterwald, J. (2015, November 23). There's more to a 'growth mindset' than assuming you have it. EdSource. Retrieved October 28, 2022, from https://edsource.org/2015/theres-more-to-a-growth-mindset-than-assuming-you-have-it/

Growth Mindset vs. fixed mindset: What's the difference? Business Insights Blog. (2022, March 10). Retrieved October 28, 2022, from https://online.hbs.edu/blog/post/growth-mindset-vs-fixed-mindset

Fixed and growth mindset. FutureLearn. (n.d.). Retrieved October 28, 2022, from https://www.futurelearn.com/info/courses/improving-study-techniques/0/steps/55541

Growth mindset vs fixed mindset: How what you think affects what you achieve. Mindset Health. (n.d.). Retrieved October 28, 2022, from https://www.mindsethealth.com/matter/growth-vs-fixed-mindset

Rapier, G. (n.d.). Steve Ballmer famously slammed the iphone - here are 12 other times bosses got it wrong on new tech. Business Insider. Retrieved October 28, 2022, from https://www.businessinsider.com/iphone-steve-ballmer-bosses-mocked-new-technologyand-got-it-wrong-2017-6

Growth Mindset In Major Companies And Resilience - CTR training. (n.d.). Retrieved October 28, 2022, from https://ctrtraining.co.uk/documents/Resilience-GPUpdate.pdf

CHAPTER FIVE

10 ways to increase your emotional intelligence | inc.com. (n.d.). Retrieved October 28, 2022, from https://www.inc.com/young-entrepreneur-council/10-ways-to-increase-your-emotional-intelligence.html

Lebow, H. I. (2021, June 7). Emotional intelligence (EQ). Psych Central. Retrieved October 28, 2022, from https://psychcentral.com/lib/what-is-emotional-intelligence-eq#examples

L;, R. P. N. J. O. (n.d.). IQ scores among homeless older adolescents: Characteristics of intellectual performance and associations with psychosocial functioning. Journal of adolescence. Retrieved October 28, 2022, from https://pubmed.ncbi.nlm.nih.gov/10462423/

León-Del-Barco, B., Lázaro, S. M., Polo-Del-Río, M.-I., & López-Ramos, V.-M. (2020, December 15). Emotional intelligence as a protective factor against victimization in school bullying. International journal of environmental research and public health. Retrieved October 28, 2022, from https://www.ncbi.nlm.nih.gov/pmc/articles/PMC7765427/

León-Pérez, J. M., Cantero-Sánchez, F. J., Fernández-Canseco, Á., & León-Rubio, J. M. (2021, October 24). Effectiveness of a humor-based training for reducing employees' distress. International journal of environmental research and public health. Retrieved October 28, 2022, from https://www.ncbi.nlm.nih.gov/pmc/articles/PMC8583317/

CHAPTER SIX

Functional Medicine Coaching Academy. (2021, May 14). Brain detox: Is it time for a cleanse? Functional Medicine Coaching Academy. Retrieved October 28, 2022, from https://functionalmedicinecoaching.org/brain-detox-is-it-time-for-a-cleanse/

Matt Walker on why sleep is your superpower. What We Seee. (2020, May 4). Retrieved September 16, 2022, from https://www.whatweseee.com/matt-walker-sleep/

REM sleep's role in Creative Solutions, Dream Inspiration and Wisdom: Matthew Walker. FoundMyFitness. (n.d.). Retrieved October 28, 2022, from https://www.foundmyfitness.com/episodes/rem-sleep-creative-solutions-dream-inspiration-wisdom

Contributors, W. M. D. E. (n.d.). Caffeine: How long do its effects last? WebMD. Retrieved September 16, 2022, from https://www.webmd.com/diet/how-long-caffeine-lasts

Saletin, J. M., Goldstein, A. N., & Walker, M. P. (2011, November). The role of sleep in directed forgetting and remembering of human memories. Cerebral cortex (New York, N.Y. : 1991).

Retrieved October 28, 2022, from https://www.ncbi.nlm.nih.gov/pmc/articles/PMC3183424/

60minutes. (2018, January 10). 60 Minutes: Brain hacking. YouTube. Retrieved October 28, 2022, from https://youtube.com/watch?v=awAMTQZmvPE

Achieving brain clearance and preventing neurodegenerative diseases—a ... (n.d.). Retrieved October 28, 2022, from https://journals.sagepub.com/doi/10.1177/0271678X20982388

G;, N. A. D. J. L. D. (n.d.). Caffeine and the central nervous system: Mechanisms of action, biochemical, metabolic and psychostimulant effects. Brain research. Brain research reviews. Retrieved October 28, 2022, from https://pubmed.ncbi.nlm.nih.gov/1356551

REM sleep's role in Creative Solutions, Dream Inspiration and Wisdom: Matthew Walker. FoundMyFitness. (n.d.). Retrieved October 28, 2022, from https://www.foundmyfitness.com/episodes/rem-sleep-creative-solutions-dream-inspiration-wisdom

Huguet, M., Payne, J. D., Kim, S. Y., & Alger, S. E. (2019, August 29). Overnight sleep benefits both neutral and negative direct associative and relational memory - cognitive, affective, & behavioral neuroscience. SpringerLink. Retrieved October 28, 2022, from https://link.springer.com/article/10.3758/s13415-019-00746-8

Saletin, J. M., Goldstein, A. N., & Walker, M. P. (2011, November). The role of sleep in directed forgetting and remembering of human memories. Cerebral cortex (New York, N.Y. : 1991). Retrieved October 28, 2022, from https://www.ncbi.nlm.nih.gov/pmc/articles/PMC3183424/

Track your sleep with Apple Watch. Apple Support. (n.d.). Retrieved September 16, 2022, from https://support.apple.com/guide/watch/sleep-apd830528336/watchos

CHAPTER SEVEN

Benefits of mindfulness. HelpGuide.org. (n.d.). Retrieved October 28, 2022, from https://www.helpguide.org/harvard/benefits-of-mindfulness.htm

Wikimedia Foundation. (2017, July 7). Talk:maharishi Mahesh Yogi/consciousness. Wikipedia. Retrieved October 28, 2022, from https://en.wikipedia.org/wiki/Talk%3AMaharishi_Mahesh_Yogi%2FConsciousness

Buddha's brain - amazon.com. (n.d.). Retrieved October 28, 2022, from https://www.amazon.com/Buddhas-Brain-Practical-Neuroscience-Happiness/dp/1491518669

6 steps to mindfulness meditation. Live Happy. (n.d.). Retrieved October 28, 2022, from https://www.livehappy.com/practice/6-steps-to-mindfulness-meditation

Davidson, R. J. (n.d.). How mindfulness changes the emotional life of our brains: Richard J. Davidson: Tedxsanfrancisco. Richard J. Davidson: How mindfulness changes the emotional life of our brains | Richard J. Davidson | TEDxSanFrancisco | TED Talk. Retrieved October 28, 2022, from https://www.ted.com/talks/richard_j_davidson_how_mindfulness_changes_the_emotional_life_of_our_brains_jan_2019

Powell, A. (2018, August 27). Harvard researchers study how mindfulness may change the brain in depressed patients. Harvard Gazette. Retrieved October 28, 2022, from https://news.harvard.edu/gazette/story/2018/04/harvard-researchers-study-how-mindfulness-may-change-the-brain-in-depressed-patients/

U.S. Department of Health and Human Services. (n.d.). Meditation and mindfulness: What you need to know. National Center for

Complementary and Integrative Health. Retrieved October 28, 2022, from https://www.nccih.nih.gov/health/meditation-and-mindfulness-what-you-need-to-know

Brady, A. (2021, August 27). 4 advanced meditation techniques and tools to deepen your practice. Chopra. Retrieved October 28, 2022, from https://chopra.com/articles/4-advanced-meditation-techniques-and-tools-to-deepen-your-practice

MediLexicon International. (n.d.). 4-7-8 breathing: How it works, benefits, and uses. Medical News Today. Retrieved October 28, 2022, from https://www.medicalnewstoday.com/articles/324417#benefits

CHAPTER EIGHT

Encyclopædia Britannica, inc. (n.d.). Napoleon summary. Encyclopædia Britannica. Retrieved October 28, 2022, from https://www.britannica.com/summary/Napoleon-I

Encyclopædia Britannica, inc. (n.d.). Napoleonic wars summary. Encyclopædia Britannica. Retrieved October 28, 2022, from https://www.britannica.com/summary/Napoleonic-Wars

Why is strategic planning important?: HBS Online. Business Insights Blog. (2020, October 6). Retrieved October 28, 2022, from https://online.hbs.edu/blog/post/why-is-strategic-planning-important

4 ways to develop your strategic thinking skills: HBS Online. Business Insights Blog. (2020, September 10). Retrieved October 28, 2022, from https://online.hbs.edu/blog/post/how-to-develop-strategic-thinking-skills

Marieforleo. (2019, September 13). Self-made millionaire: The simple strategy that helped increase my odds of success by 42%. CNBC. Retrieved October 28, 2022, from https://www.cnbc.com/2019/09/13/self-made-millionaire-how-to-increase-your-odds-of-success-by-42-percent-marie-forleo.html

Elle Kaplan. (2017, November 21). 3 smart habits that will improve your wealth and success this month. Elle Kaplan. Retrieved October 28, 2022, from https://ellekaplan.com/3-smart-habits-will-improve-wealth-success-month/

Elle Kaplan. (2017, August 22). 3 behaviors that will put you on the path to Success. Elle Kaplan. Retrieved October 28, 2022, from https://ellekaplan.com/3-behaviors-will-put-path-success/

Elle Kaplan. (2017, August 22). 3 behaviors that will put you on the path to Success. Elle Kaplan. Retrieved October 28, 2022, from https://ellekaplan.com/3-behaviors-will-put-path-success/

CHAPTER NINE

Hogan, C. (2020, April 30). How to switch out of your default mode and live from your advanced settings. Medium. Retrieved October 28, 2022, from https://medium.com/@cchogan1/how-to-switch-out-of-your-default-mode-and-live-from-your-advanced-settings-d59b64a55a23

Getaway. (2020, July 7). Read about the default mode network: Getaway. Getaway Journal. Retrieved October 28, 2022, from https://journal.getaway.house/default-mode-network-your-mind-at-rest/

Haddadeen, S. (2022, September 24). Psilocybin and the default mode network. Microdose. Retrieved October 28, 2022, from https://www.microdosebros.com/psilocybin-and-the-default-mode-network/#:

Li, W., Mai, X., & Liu, C. (1AD, January 1). The default mode network and social understanding of others: What do brain connectivity studies tell us. Frontiers. Retrieved October 28, 2022, from https://www.frontiersin.org/articles/10.3389/fnhum.2014.00074/full

Forster, P. (2021, June 24). Default mode network and depression treatment - ketamine and TMS. Gateway Psychiatric. Retrieved

October 28, 2022, from https://www.gatewaypsychiatric.com/default-mode-network-and-depression/

Koselka, E. P. D., Weidner, L. C., Minasov, A., Berman, M. G., Leonard, W. R., Santoso, M. V., de Brito, J. N., Pope, Z. C., Pereira, M. A., & Horton, T. H. (2019, November 7). Walking green: Developing an evidence base for nature prescriptions. International journal of environmental research and public health. Retrieved October 28, 2022, from https://www.ncbi.nlm.nih.gov/pmc/articles/PMC6888434/

Akiki TJ;Averill CL;Wrocklage KM;Scott JC;Averill LA;Schweinsburg B;Alexander-Bloch A;Martini B;Southwick SM;Krystal JH;Abdallah CG; (n.d.). Default mode network abnormalities in posttraumatic stress disorder: A novel network-restricted topology approach. NeuroImage. Retrieved October 28, 2022, from https://pubmed.ncbi.nlm.nih.gov/29730491/

Kirchner, B. (2018, July 18). TPN vs. DMN - neural mechanisms and mindfulness. Exploring The Business Brain. Retrieved October 28, 2022, from https://exploringthebusinessbrain.com/tpn-vs-dmn-neural-mechanisms-mindfulness/

CHAPTER TEN

WebMD. (n.d.). Famous people with ADHD / ADD: 13 celebrities with ADHD / add. WebMD. Retrieved October 28, 2022, from https://www.webmd.com/add-adhd/ss/slideshow-celebrities-add-adhd

Holland, K. (2020, March 25). Celebrities with ADHD: 9 famous people with ADHD. Healthline. Retrieved October 28, 2022, from https://www.healthline.com/health/adhd/celebrities#1.-Michael-Phelps

Holland, K. (2020, March 25). Celebrities with ADHD: 9 famous people with ADHD. Healthline. Retrieved October 28, 2022, from https://www.healthline.com/health/adhd/celebrities

Kernbach, J. M., Satterthwaite, T. D., Bassett, D. S., Smallwood, J., Margulies, D., Krall, S., Shaw, P., Varoquaux, G., Thirion, B., Konrad, K., & Bzdok, D. (2018, July 17). Shared endo-phenotypes of default mode dysfunction in attention deficit/hyperactivity disorder and autism spectrum disorder. Nature News. Retrieved October 28, 2022, from https://www.nature.com/articles/s41398-018-0179-6

What is ADHD? Psychiatry.org - What is ADHD? (n.d.). Retrieved October 28, 2022, from https://www.psychiatry.org/patients-families/adhd/what-is-adhd

Fox, K. C. R., Nijeboer, S., Dixon, M. L., Floman, J. L., Ellamil, M., Rumak, S. P., Sedlmeier, P., & Christoff, K. (2014, April 3). Is meditation associated with altered brain structure? A systematic review and meta-analysis of morphometric neuroimaging in meditation practitioners. Neuroscience & Biobehavioral Reviews. Retrieved October 28, 2022, from https://www.sciencedirect.com/science/article/pii/S0149763414000724

NHS. (n.d.). ADHD Diagnosis. NHS choices. Retrieved October 28, 2022, from https://www.nhs.uk/conditions/attention-deficit-hyperactivity-disorder-adhd/diagnosis/

Schimelpfening, N. (2022, July 23). Dialectical behavior therapy (DBT): Definition, techniques, and efficacy. Verywell Mind. Retrieved October 28, 2022, from https://www.verywellmind.com/dialectical-behavior-therapy-1067402

Kasuya-Ueba, Y., Zhao, S., & Toichi, M. (1AD, January 1). The effect of music intervention on attention in children: Experimental evidence. Frontiers. Retrieved October 28, 2022, from

https://www.frontiersin.org/articles/10.3389/fnins.2020.0075
7/full

Benefits of Music for General Public. Listen4Life Foundation.
(n.d.). Retrieved October 28, 2022, from
https://www.listenforlife.org/healing-benefits.html

Kollins, D. S. (n.d.). Video-game therapy may help treat ADHD,
study finds. ABC News. Retrieved October 28, 2022, from
https://abcnews.go.com/Health/video-game-therapy-treat-
adhd-study-finds/story?id=69186285

Is therapy using horses effective for ADHD? CHADD. (2019,
February 28). Retrieved October 28, 2022, from
https://chadd.org/adhd-weekly/is-therapy-using-horses-
effective-for-adhd/

Boddy-Evans, M. (2019, February 20). The effect of "Right brain
left brain" on art. LiveAbout. Retrieved October 28, 2022, from
https://www.liveabout.com/right-brain-left-brain-theory-art-
2579156

Kasuya-Ueba, Y., Zhao, S., & Toichi, M. (1AD, January 1). The effect
of music intervention on attention in children: Experimental
evidence. Frontiers. Retrieved October 28, 2022, from
https://www.frontiersin.org/articles/10.3389/fnins.2020.0075
7/full

WebMD. (n.d.). Proceed with caution: 10 things you should
consider before stopping your ADHD meds. WebMD. Retrieved
October 28, 2022, from https://www.webmd.com/add-
adhd/ss/cm/10-things-you-should-consider-before-stopping-
adhd-meds

CLOSING THOUGHTS

Xplore. (n.d.). Walt Disney quotes. BrainyQuote. Retrieved
October 28, 2022, from
https://www.brainyquote.com/quotes/walt_disney_163027